The cornerstone new building of Jordan Marsh was laid in 1949 at the corner of Chauncy Street, *on the left*, and Summer Street. The building was designed by the noted Boston architectural firm of Perry, Shaw, Kehoe and Dean and was to be built for the centennial of Jordan Marsh Company. Impressive in its design, the use of red brick and Ionic pilasters were a decided nod to Boston's architectural legacy.

JORDAN MARSH

New England's Largest Store

ANTHONY M. SAMMARCO

THE
History
PRESS

Published by The History Press
Charleston, SC
www.historypress.net

All images are from the author's collection unless otherwise noted.

Page 1: An early trade card of Jordan Marsh & Co. was used from the turn of the twentieth century, when it was adopted by Eben Dyer Jordan Jr., who served as president of the store from 1895 to 1916. An armored metal-clad arm holds a dagger aloft with two winged griffins holding the quartered shield of Jordan Marsh & Co.

First published 2017

Manufactured in the United States

ISBN 9781467137904

Library of Congress Control Number: 2017948452

For Cesidio "Joe" Cedrone

Behind this façade lies a story—the romance of a great New England institution. It is worth telling. It should be worth reading. In the hope that the public may find it so, it is here set down.

There's a time for looking backward and a time for looking forward
—Eben Dyer Jordan

CONTENTS

ACKNOWLEDGEMENTS

The Jordan Marsh Company was a one-of-a-kind department store in Boston that seemed to offer to the public everything under the sun attractively displayed in its many acres of display space. After 1951, when its first suburban department store was opened at Shoppers World on Route 9 in Framingham, Massachusetts, the store was to evolve as a thriving department store chain with stores throughout New England and also throughout Florida. In the research and writing of this book, many people were very kind to share their memories and stories of this once fabled place, and I would like to thank them as well as the following people and institutions:

Susan Agaman; Anthony Artuso, Association of the First Corps of Cadets; Hope Lincoln Baker; the *Barnstable Patriot*, Debi Boucher-Stetson; Kathleen Walsh Beirne; Susan T. Belekewicz; Joan Bentinck-Smith; Mary G. Blake; the Boston Athenaeum, Catharina Slautterback; Boston Public Library, Henry Scannell, Research Services, with tremendous thanks; Charles Boston, Shopping Days in Retro Boston Blog; Alan Bourbeau; Sally Bradshaw; Ellen Bragalone; Karen Buscemi; John Canesi; Dolley Carlson; Elizabeth Carroll-Horrocks, Head of Special Collections, State Library of Massachusetts; Maureen McQuillen Cater; Calvary Cemetery, Boston; Hutchinson and Lina Cedmarco; Cesidio "Joe" Cedrone; Reverend Ellen Chahey and Edward Maroney; Michael Chesson; Dr. John and Lortetta Christoforo; Elise Ciregna and Stephen LoPiccolo; Barbara Clark; Edie Clifford; Colortek of Boston, Jackie Anderson and Jimmy Kwong; William

The Jordan Marsh Company corner tower with its massive clock was designed by Bradlee, Winslow & Wetherall and built in 1881 adjacent to the store designed on the left by Nathaniel J. Bradlee. At the turn of the twentieth century, the junction of Washington and Avon Street (formerly Avon Place) was called "the busiest corner on Boston's busiest street."

and Frances Bellantoni Condaxis; Kaitlin Connolly; Therese Desmond and Meg Toyias, Milton Cemetery; Sal and Mary DiDomenico; Thomas Dunlay; Sandra Eaton; the marvelous world of eBay; Alberta Elias; Mary Anne English; Rosemary Donovan Finn; Barbara Smith Fitzgerald; Nancy Flemming; Forest Hills Cemetery, George Milley, Janice Stetz and

Sally Alves; Charles Fraser; Greg French; Katherine Hickey Fulham; Vin Gandolfo; Bob Ganno; Jeannette Genova; Ann Colgan Gillis; Edward W. Gordon; Mary Ethel Grady; Jack Grinold; Donna Halper; John F. Hanafin; Helen Hannon; John P. Hickey Jr.; Steve Hill; Karen Hilliard; Chip Hilton; Historical Society of Cheshire County, New Hampshire; Historic New England, Lorna Condon; Hofmann-Figuen, Reinhard Hofmann, Martin Hofmann and Doreen Wieland; Martin and Deborah Blackman Jacobs; Jacqueline M. Jacquiot; Bradley Jay, WBZ 1030 Radio; the "Jordan Marsh" Facebook page; Stephen Kharfen; Donna Korman; Susan Greendyke Lachevre; Richard Leccese; Lauren Leja; Robin Liftman; Erica Lindamood, Old South Meeting House, Boston; Edward Mack, my initial editor; Dorothy V. Malcolm; Martin Manning; Constance L. Martin; Denis McGrath; Theresa McKillop; Nancy Dyer Mitton; the Mitton family; Alice Dick Moran; Hilda M. Morrill; Dee Morris; Mount Auburn Cemetery, Meg Winslow; Eddie Mulkern; Eileen Mullen; Dennis O'Brien; Pat O'Mara; Orleans Camera; Stephen Owens; James Pardy; Stanley Paine, Stanley J. Paine Auctioneers; Mary E. Paul; Linda Pennington; Loumona Petroff; Richard Philpott; Christine Puccia; Lilian M.C. Randall; Robin H. Ray; Jordan Rich, WBZ 1030 Radio; Ann Pistorino Russell; Louise Russell; Dr. Dean Saluti and Marjorie Cahn; Richard Salvucci and Leslie Lehmann; Maria Saxe; Kimberly Effgen Sliney; J. Banks Smither, my editor; Special Collections Archives in the Massachusetts State House; Judith Sumner; Carolyn Thornton; Kenneth Turino and Chris Mathias; Warren Turino; University of Massachusetts, Archives and Special Collections, Joseph P. Healy Library, Boston, Joanne Riley and Andrew Elder; Grace Wagner, Massachusetts Historical Society; Ann and Thomas Walsh; Daniel White; Ellen and Thomas White; Nancy White; Lewis Whitlock; Jodiann Wise; and Cathryn A. Wright.

Though Jordan Marsh had stores throughout Florida; in Albany, New York; Bedford, New Hampshire; Portland, Maine; and Warwick, Rhode Island, this book primarily deals with the flagship store in Boston and its suburban stores throughout New England from 1851 to 1995.

INTRODUCTION

Founded in 1851 by partners Eben Dyer Jordan and Benjamin Lloyd Marsh, Jordan and Marsh opened its first store with a capital of $5,000 on Milk Street in Boston selling linens, silks, cottons, calicoes, ribbons and assorted dry goods to discriminating Victorian Bostonians. Following the Civil War, after which the business had dramatically increased and additional space was needed, the store was successively moved to the Cruft Building on Pearl Street and then to the Free Stone Building at Winthrop Square and later to Washington Street, between Summer and Avon Streets. In the latter location, in its impressive five-story brownstone store designed by Nathaniel J. Bradlee, they unveiled the novel concept of "department shopping" all under one roof.

Jordan and Marsh were thought of as skillful and enterprising entrepreneurs, and they would rapidly expand their business. By 1861, the partners had begun to sell directly to the public rather than remaining as strictly dry goods wholesalers, and thus they began to offer an even more diverse and unparalleled variety of goods that augmented their store and dramatically increased their sales and profit. Eben Dyer Jordan would travel as early as 1853 to Europe in search of fine linens, silks, woolens and unique housewares from around the world that could be sold to Bostonians and augment the selection of what was usually available from other local stores. From the mid-nineteenth century on, Jordan Marsh was to offer a tremendous selection of goods that included such things as men's, women's and children's clothing and accessories, including collars, cuffs, shawls and

Eben Dyer Jordan (1822–1895) was the co-founder with Benjamin Lloyd Marsh (1823–1865) of Jordan and Marsh in 1851. It was said of the partners that they "excelled through character, knowledge of the business, courage and genius for hard work." Jordan and Marsh were skillful and enterprising entrepreneurs, and they would rapidly expand their business from wholesale to retail.

sports outfits, parasols and umbrellas, furs and jewelry; furniture; art and antiques; trunks and travel bags; children's toys; and oriental carpets that attracted captivated shoppers six days a week. Jordan Marsh even boasted of having the "exclusive right to sell at retail in Boston the Black Silk Ribbons of the well known Lyons Manufacturers, 'Les Fils' de C.J. Bonnet & Co.," and some of the fabrics for boys' suits were made exclusively for Jordan Marsh & Co. by one of the leading manufactories of Galashiel, Scotland. The celebrated Fleur de Lis Corsets were proclaimed by advertisements to be "made by the best hands in Paris." The store offered personal service, with the impressive adage that the customer is always right, along with easy credit, art exhibitions and musical performances—all of which brought the ever-increasing numbers of customers from near and far. It soon became a treasured part of middle-class life for shoppers, who went to town and shopped in the elegantly appointed department store that offered a wide array of interesting and reasonably priced merchandise.

Jordan Marsh, by the turn of the twentieth century, was not just the largest department store in New England, but it also offered unrivaled services to its shoppers and those who had store charges. The unheard-of money-back guarantee if a customer was not pleased with her purchase was to secure a loyal clientele who patronized the store; actually, the store was quoted as promising that "perfect satisfaction would be given, or the money would be refunded." In fact, customers who encountered difficulties, no matter how trivial, were urged to contact the complaint bureau. Of course, with the addition of Eben Dyer Jordan Jr. and Edward J. Mitton in the 1880s, the store continued to offer quality goods but also began the modernization of the store with new technological advancements such as electric lights that were to transform shopping, the telephone, elevators and a series of

The Jordan Marsh delivery wagon, seen here in the mid-1870s, had six horses that would pull the wagon through the streets of Boston after the Civil War. The delivery wagon is bedecked with flowers and surrounded by top-hatted men, as it may have been decorated for the Boston parade held in honor of the centennial of the United States in 1876, as well as the twenty-fifth anniversary of the store's founding.

pneumatic tubes that sent both cash and credit slips from the departments to the offices. Each of these aspects of modern technology made Jordan Marsh an exciting as well as novel destination in Boston.

Justifiably called the "largest, most progressive and most liberal department store in New England," Jordan Marsh catered to its shoppers and offered such comforts as well-appointed waiting rooms, which had comfortable chairs, rockers and desks where one could use store stationery to send notes while awaiting family and friends; a secure storage room for packages for busy shoppers; and a soda fountain where refreshing drinks and dishes of ice cream were served, as well as a bakery where the now famous Jordan Marsh blueberry muffin was offered and rarely refused by shoppers who returned home with a box tied with red-and-white string.

Managers, buyers and staff seemed to work in unison to ensure that Jordan Marsh was not just a destination but a place that embraced its preeminence in the city. By the turn of the twentieth century, the store was reputed to have a mailing list of over 100,000 names to whom lavishly illustrated multi-page catalogues were mailed in the spring and the fall that showcased the wide

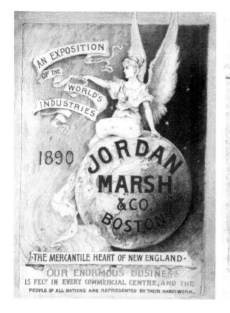 

Left: The cover of the 1890 Jordan Marsh & Co. catalogue claimed, "Our enormous business is felt in every commercial center, and the people of all nations are represented by their handiwork." A winged woman sits on the terrestrial globe as a ribbon flutters from her hand, proclaiming "An Exposition of the world's industries" in the mercantile heart of New England.

Right: An advertisement of Jordan Marsh from 1872 shows the Washington Street store façade, which was proclaimed by flags on the roof to be "in the heart of the city," with banners stretched across the façade offering furniture salesrooms, parlor, library, dining room, chamber, bedding and kitchens under one roof. Notice the horse-drawn carriages that proclaimed the store served the "Carriage Trade" of Boston.

array of merchandise that was available. One could either shop in the store or place an order by telephone, telegraph or mail for items that would either be delivered or sent by parcel post. As the store stated in these catalogues, customers could save money by ordering merchandise from the comfort of their homes rather than traveling to Boston, which would cost far more than mailing an order form. It was also said that any errors would be promptly remedied whenever they occurred and that satisfaction was guaranteed. Jordan Marsh & Co., as the store was known after 1861, was to cater to a new and more sophisticated generation of shoppers who had come to expect the high quality of service that was consistently offered, and when it failed to meet the expectations of the public, the store would promptly remedy whatever mistake or disappointment might have occurred. This, in itself, not only pleased the buying public but also ensured their continued loyalty.

By the mid-twentieth century—under the long direction of George W. Mitton from 1916 to 1930 and Richard Mitton and Edward R. Mitton, who served as successive presidents—Jordan Marsh had evolved as an anchor in downtown Boston and one of almost a dozen prominent and popular department stores that offered a wide array of quality goods. However, though it may have been the largest of the department stores in the city with some two acres of display space in five buildings, it still utilized newspaper advertising and sales as a major way to induce the public to shop in the store. Following World War II, Jordan Marsh envisioned a new modern addition that had all the major accoutrements that would appeal to the general public: automatic doorways, air conditioning, electric escalators and radiant heated sidewalks that fronted onto huge plate-glass display windows that were designed to be a city block in size. The prominent Boston architectural firm of Perry, Shaw, Kehoe and Dean was commissioned to design a massive two-part addition that was designed as an updated Colonial Revival design

The 1958 ribbon cutting at the new Jordan Marsh store at the Northshore Shopping Center in Peabody, Massachusetts, shows, *from left to right*, Cameron S. Thompson, vice president; Houston Rawls, president of National Planning and Research; Newton L. Walzer, vice president; Philip C. O'Donnell, mayor of Peabody; James V. Keddy, general manager of the Northshore store; Edward R. Mitton, president of Jordan Marsh; B. Earl Puckett, chairman of Allied Stores; M.T. Rhodes, director of Northshore Shopping Mall; and John Volpe, president of Volpe Construction Company.

On opening day in 1956 at the new Jordan Marsh Warehouse in Auburndale, Massachusetts, are Newton mayor Howard J. Whitmore Jr. on the left and Edward Richardson Mitton, president of Jordan Marsh, standing behind a "Royal Chef" rotisserie. This new warehouse greatly expanded the storage of merchandise to be delivered throughout New England.

The new Jordan Marsh store at Shoppers World on Route 9 in Framingham, Massachusetts, was opened in 1951 and had an ample parking lot with the ascendancy of the automobile after World War II. Said to be the "World's Largest and Most Beautiful Shopping Center," the dome of the Jordan Marsh store was considered the third largest in the world, after the Vatican in Rome and St. Paul's Cathedral in London.

with red brick and wood Ionic pilasters and lintels that created an impressive corner with a multistory, curved mullioned window at Chauncy and Summer Streets that not only added to the economic revitalization of the downtown but also created a fitting and modern space for the upcoming centennial festivities of Jordan Marsh in 1951.

However, by 1951, Jordan Marsh was also to begin the expansion of its store to the suburbs, with its first branch store being opened on October 4, 1951, at Shoppers World on Route 9 in Framingham, Massachusetts. This expansion was due to the ascendancy of the automobile. As the urban public, following World War II, began to move to the suburbs in record numbers thanks to both the GI Loan and rapid suburban residential development, the store was affected. Because of the rapid expansion, it was to become by the 1970s not just the largest department store in New England but also the largest department store chain in the United States.

Many people mourned when Jordan Marsh was closed in 1995 and the Macy's name replaced it on the venerable façades of the Jordan Marsh stores. This book chronicles the steady and determined growth of Jordan Marsh from its founding in 1851 to 1995 and also tells of its fascinating and ever-evolving history as Boston's first true department store.

Chapter 1

Eben Dyer Jordan and Benjamin Lloyd Marsh

Co-founders of Jordan Marsh Company

*They excelled through character, knowledge of the business,
courage and genius for hard work.*

Eben Dyer Jordan and Benjamin Lloyd Marsh, the two men who in 1851 would join as partners to create a dry goods store known as Jordan and Marsh, were fairly successful merchants in the 1840s who each kept a small dry goods store on Hanover Street in Boston's North End. Hanover Street is one of the oldest streets in the city of Boston and was originally an Indian footpath that became known as Orange Tree Lane and would eventually be extended to include both Middle and North Streets so that it stretched from Court (now known as Cambridge) Street in the West End to Lynn (now known as Commercial) Street on the waterfront. In 1708, the street was renamed after the Royal House of Hanover, heirs to the British throne under the Act of Settlement 1701, which began the rule of six monarchs from George I to Victoria. This royal family ruled the American colonies, of which Massachusetts Bay Colony was a part until 1776. The North End was a densely settled neighborhood even in the seventeenth and eighteenth centuries, but after the city of Boston was incorporated in 1822, the North End neighborhood embraced a changing streetscape with the beginnings of the immigration tide in the mid-nineteenth century.

At the time of the Civil War, the North End had retained since the eighteenth century a distinctly mercantile economy that dealt with shipping, trading and all aspects of life along the waterfront. The Seaman's

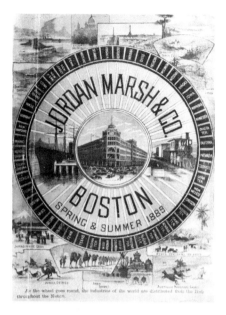

The Jordan Marsh & Co. 1889 Spring and Summer catalogue cover stated, "As the wheel goes round, the industries of the world are distributed from the Hub [as the city of Boston was known] throughout the Nation." Whether distributed by ship or railroad, goods were sent to the states and territories of the United States from Jordan Marsh, seen in the center.

Aid Society of the City of Boston was a charity founded in Boston in 1833 to help improve the welfare of seamen and their families, especially while the seamen were at sea. The Mariner's House in North Square was opened by the Boston Port Society and provided affordable rooms on a daily or weekly basis, meals, a library and daily morning and evening prayers led by Father Taylor for sailors during short stays between ships. The Seaman's Bethel, also in North Square and opposite the Mariner's House, was opened by Reverend Edward Thompson Taylor (1793–1871), fondly known as Father Taylor, a former sailor turned preacher. Father Taylor became the first minister of Seaman's Bethel, which was founded in 1829 by the Port Society of Boston. Seaman's Bethel ministered to the seamen who were vulnerable to the temptations and dangers of the nineteenth-century Boston waterfront. Father Taylor's unique sermons, delivered in the salty language and imagery of a sailor, were to ensure a widespread reputation throughout the city, and the Seaman's Bethel gathered a large following of ardent supporters. The bustling aspect of Hanover Street and the adjacent North Square was further increased when the American House hotel was built in 1835 and became one of the more popular hotels in the city. The streets were thronged throughout the day and night, with ships arriving daily at wharves projecting into Boston Harbor and bringing not just sailors but also passengers who added to the hubbub.

The Jordan Marsh & Co. 1887 Summer catalogue said, "We invite correspondence from all parts of THE WORLD." Cherubs reach for and gather the correspondence that falls from a mail opening above that had radiating state names, from which the correspondence had been sent to the Mail Order Department.

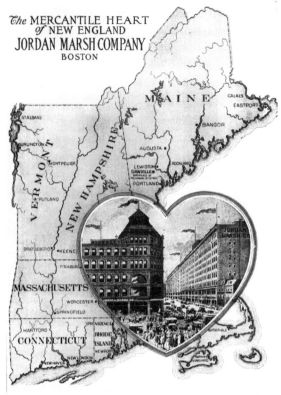

Left: Jordan Marsh Company claimed that it was literally as well as figuratively "the mercantile heart of New England," with the Main Store and Annex flanking Avon Street at Washington Street, all depicted within a red-lined heart overlaid on a map of New England.

Below: Looking north on Washington Street from Avon Street on the right, "The Shopping Hour" at noon in Boston had the streets thronged, with pedestrians going about their business and the streetcars that networked transportation throughout the city. Notice the bronze tablet on the left that declares it to be "the busiest corner on Boston's busiest street."

Among the shops along Hanover Street was that of Eben Dyer Jordan (who, in 1841, opened his store at 146 Hanover Street at the corner of Mechanics Lane) and Benjamin Lloyd Marsh (whose store Marsh and Bartlett, later to be known as Marsh & Co., was located just down the street at 168 Hanover Street). Undoubtedly, the two men were well acquainted as near neighbors, but in the book *Tales of the Observer*, it was said that Jordan, who left his job as an errand boy in the dry goods store of William P. Tenney & Co., was set up in business by the merchant Joshua Stetson, who decided that because of his commendable work ethic, Jordan was certainly "worth a financial risk." Jordan made the decision to open his new dry goods store before dawn to serve the people who had taken the early packets that docked in Boston Harbor. He boarded nearby at Mrs. Hadaway's on Sheafe Street in the North End, and on his first day, he arrived at the shop at 4:00 a.m. to be greeted by Louisa Bareiss, his very first customer, who would purchase a yard of cherry-colored ribbon. The rest has become part of the history of Boston. Jordan did extremely well, and in 1847, he sold his business and joined James Madison Bebee as clerk to learn the dry goods business "more thoroughly and in a larger way." He probably felt confident enough of his business and salesmanship ability, as on January 20, 1851, Eben Dyer Jordan and Benjamin Lloyd Marsh went into partnership as Jordan and Marsh with a store at 129 Milk Street in Boston, where their stalwart business platform was "The better you serve your customers, the better you serve yourself."

Chapter 2

Victorian Boston in the Age of Jordan Marsh

The better you serve your customers, the better you serve yourself.
—*Jordan and Marsh, 1851*

In 1851, Jordan and Marsh was founded by Eben Dyer Jordan and Benjamin Lloyd Marsh at 129 Milk Street as a jobbing business in dry goods. Both partners had been fairly successful in their own businesses in the previous decade and had brought business acumen that would serve them well over the next few years, but as an early history of the store states, "They multiplied that several times by their characters, knowledge of the business, courage and genius for hard work."

Jordan and Marsh grew in business and reputation in Boston, and in 1853, Eben Jordan made his first trip to Europe to enter the foreign buying field. As *The Story of a Store* said, "This was the beginning of the house's connection with European manufacturers. It enabled them to buy their imported goods at first cost, and the business relations that were then formed have enabled the firm to get their goods at bottom prices and also in many cases to secure exclusive control of many desirable lines of foreign merchandise." The store was moved in 1856 to larger quarters on Pearl Street, where it occupied the Cruft Block at 16, 18, 20 and 22 Pearl Street. This step was tempered by the Panic of 1857, which had a devastating effect on business in the city of Boston. However, by tightening belts and promptly settling their accounts with creditors, at a tremendous financial loss to the fledgling company, they were able to stem the tide and miraculously survive. In fact, they survived

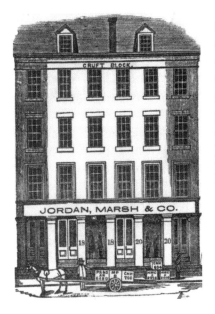

The Cruft Block, named for Isaac S. Cruft, was at 18 and 20 Pearl Street in Boston and was the location of Jordan and Marsh in 1856. The buildings on either side (16 and 22 Pearl Street) were later to be incorporated into the growing business until it was moved to Winthrop Square to the Free Stone Building.

the panic when other businesses failed, and it was said by an English supplier of the company's remarkable survival that "you ought to have a monument for your pluck in preferring honor to profits." The business continued to expand, and in 1859, it moved to the Free Stone Building at 148 and 154 Devonshire Street in Winthrop Square. This six-story building with 14,400 square feet of floor space was said to be not just impressive but "at that time had no superior in the country." The location, between Franklin and Summer Streets, was convenient, and the area, which had once been a fashionable residential neighborhood, had given way to commerce by the late 1850s.

The company during this time had not just increased in annual sales but had begun a public relations strategy that publicized what it was doing. At the outbreak of the Civil War, Jordan Marsh & Co.—as it had been renamed in 1852 when Charles Marsh and later Henry W. Taylor joined the company—had the first flag raising from a flagpole that surmounted the store, and to the male employees who wished to enlist in the Union army, the store owners offered "the cost of their outfit, agreeing to pay their salaries during their absence and to retain their positions" until they had served their period of service. No other company could compare to the generosity of Jordan Marsh & Co., and it was readily noticed by Bostonians. After the Civil War ended in 1865, there was a movement to have a Peace Jubilee in Boston. It was thought that music might heal the divide in the United States. A pavilion was built in the newly created Back Bay of Boston, roughly at the present junction of St. James Avenue and Dartmouth Street, where the famous composer and bandmaster Patrick Sarsfield Gilmore led a series of musical extravaganzas that had "a chorus of 23,000 voices, an orchestra of 1,000 pieces, the most famous bands and singers in the world and audiences of 100,000 people."

People came from near and far. Eben Dyer Jordan served not only as a major promoter but also as treasurer of the Peace Jubilee and was also a major donor to the event; it was said at the time that without his name and personal exertions, it would not have been the success it was.

In 1861, Jordan Marsh & Co.—which by this time had been increased by Charles Marsh, the younger brother of Benjamin Marsh; Henry W. Taylor; and James Fisk Jr. as junior partners—acquired the retail business of George W. Warren Company, which was on Washington Street, between Summer and Avon Streets. The store had been built for developer William Turrell Andrews, who in 1859 had commissioned noted Boston architect Nathaniel J. Bradlee to design a new four-story store with a dormered Mansard roof that was the epitome of elegance and was to begin the transformation of the area into large dry goods stores. This new location, in addition to the store at Winthrop Square and offices at 184–86 Church Street in New York, greatly expanded the business, but by 1871, the partners had decided to consolidate their business at the Washington Street store. This was providential, as the following year the Great Boston Fire of 1872 destroyed forty acres of Boston from the area of Summer Street to Washington Street to Milk Street and the waterfront, including Winthrop Square. Though only a block away, Jordan Marsh & Co. remarkably survived the devastating fire and began a rapid expansion of the business to surrounding buildings until 1880, when the lot at the corner of Washington and Avon Streets, adjacent to the former Warren store, was purchased and the prominent Boston architectural firm of Bradlee, Winslow & Wetherall was commissioned to build a five-story brownstone store with a six-story tower surmounted by a massive clock that quickly became known as the "busiest corner on Boston's busiest street." With ground-floor plate-glass display windows that were often changed to highlight seasonal clothing and accessories, the tower had three massive two-story arched windows that often had models promenading and displaying the latest fashions that

Jordan Marsh & Co. advertised as "Importers of Foreign and dealers in American Dry Goods" at 148 and 154 Devonshire Street at Winthrop Square. This trade card from 1861 shows founders Eben D. Jordan and Benjamin L. Marsh joined by junior partners Charles Marsh and James Fisk Jr.

could be seen by pedestrians below. The store was now truly a "department store" in that there were separate departments offering everything from women's, men's and children's clothing to household furnishing, carpets, draperies, toys and dozens of other things that Victorian Bostonians could marvel at—all under one roof with over two acres of display space.

It was thought that Jordan Marsh & Co. was the first department store. As said in *Economics of Retailing*:

> *Whatever were the beginnings of department stores, the fact remains that the period following the panic of 1873–4 in this country saw a rapid development of this class of retailing establishment. The Jordan Marsh Company's store in Boston is credited by some with being the first. This store, it is understood, borrowed the idea from Bon Marche, a large retail store in Paris, and the first department store of which anything is known anywhere. Shortly after the Jordan Marsh store had been departmentalized, other department stores were established in Chicago, Philadelphia, and New York.*

The new Jordan Marsh building attracted great attention in Boston, and in an article published in 1884 in the *Boston Post*, it was said that Jordan Marsh & Co. now had "the finest and most colossal store the world ever saw, surpassing by far anything that had been attempted either in New York or Philadelphia up to that time." Eben Dyer Jordan continued to expand and increase his business even though his stalwart partner Benjamin L. Marsh had died in 1865. Charles Marsh would continue as a junior partner until his death in 1886 (Taylor and Fiske left after only a few years). In 1870, James Clark Jordan joined Jordan Marsh & Co., followed in 1881 by Eben Dyer Jordan Jr.; both were sons of the founder. In this period from 1880 to 1900, the business was to become the leading department store in New England, with many shoppers realizing that its merchandise was to be found nowhere else and was representative of the best that buyers could supply. In fact, Jordan Marsh Company referred to the store as being the literal "Mercantile Heart of New England." With the obvious confidence of the public that realized the quality for the money, the store expanded again in 1898 when a new eight-story building called the Annex was erected at Avon, Chauncy and Bedford Streets; it was often referred to as the Furniture Building. Here not just furniture but also household furnishings, including carpets, lamps, art pottery and draperies, were offered to the middle- and upper-class Bostonians who lived in the city and in the recently annexed cities and

Charles Marsh (1829–1886) was the younger brother of Benjamin Lloyd Marsh and was a junior partner of Jordan Marsh Company for many years. He had charge of the wholesale department, which was under his personal supervision. He initially lived at 58 Boylston Street in Boston but in 1878 moved to 35 Commonwealth Avenue in Boston's Back Bay.

The tower building at the corner of Washington Street and Avon Street was designed by Bradlee, Winslow & Wetherall and was added to the five-story building seen to the left, which was designed by Nathaniel J. Bradlee for William T. Andrews and occupied by the George W. Warren Company until it was purchased in 1861 by Jordan Marsh Company. The two buildings created one of the most impressive streetscapes in the city of Boston.

The earliest known charge token issued by Jordan Marsh Company dated to the early 1880s and had the intertwined initials of the company in a circular surround with two crossed hilted swords, all of which was surmounted by a coronet. On the reverse was the assigned number for the customer. Extending credit to customers was to greatly increase the business of the company and allowed it to greatly expand.

towns that surrounded Boston. In 1868, the city of Roxbury was annexed to Boston, followed by the town of Dorchester in 1870, the city of Charlestown in 1874, the town of Brighton in 1874 and the town of West Roxbury (which included the neighborhoods of Jamaica Plain and Roslindale) in 1874. It would not be until 1912 that the town of Hyde Park was annexed to Boston, thereby creating city neighborhoods that were rapidly developed with new housing that brought residents to the city seeking household furnishings and accessories. This new Annex was connected to the Main Store by a marble-lined walkway referred to as the "subway" that tunneled under Avon Street and allowed shoppers to cross from one building to another in all weather.

In 1907, after a fire destroyed buildings adjacent to the Annex, plans were made for the company to build a new building adjacent to the Annex at the opposite corner of Washington and Avon Streets. This nine-story fireproof building was completed four years later and was known as the New Building. This new addition to Jordan Marsh Company—the name adopted in 1901—was to effectively double the space available for displays and department counters and had a two-story basement. It was said in *The Story of a Store* that with the

> *completion of the New Building and the consequent moving of the Silverware, Jewelry, Leather Goods, Books, Stationery, Toilet Goods, China, Glassware and Music into this building [it] gave the necessary space in the Main Store so that a complete remodeling could be undertaken in the latter. The aisles were widened, the space allotted the different parts of the business was increased; old stock rooms and packing rooms*

were torn out; a complete Men's Store was established on the street floor; carpets were laid and thousands of dollars were spent on new fixtures. The transformation was finished and wonderful; a change from an old-time mercantile establishment into a big, broad, roomy retail store confining itself to the sale of dry goods, dress accessories and apparel for men, women and children, with by far the largest stocks of their kind to be found in New England. With two great buildings—one devoted to house furnishings and the other to dry goods and kindred lines—the arrangement offers the most convenient manner of classifying stocks for easy selection by customers.

In 1910, Jordan Marsh Company opened the Basement Store, which was under both buildings and had over 100,000 square feet of sales space. The Basement Store was advertised as being "larger than most department stores in medium sized cities...and was for the sale of less expensive lines of goods." Obviously Eben Dyer Jordan Jr. and Edward J. Mitton, partners of Jordan Marsh Company, were well aware of the Filene's Automatic Bargain Basement that had opened the previous year and its success in offering

The impressive seven-story Jordan Marsh Wholesale Store was designed by Bradlee, Winslow & Wetherall and built in 1889 at 69 Bedford Street, at the curved corner of Kingston and Bedford Streets. It offered wholesale prices on Jordan Marsh merchandise.

Eben Dyer Jordan (1822–1895) was painted by Jean-Joseph Benjamin-Constant, and the massive portrait hung in the stair hall of the Main Store, just opposite the entrance at Washington Street and Avon Street. Today, the massive gilt-framed portrait hangs in the Commonwealth Salon of the Boston Public Library at Copley Square in Boston.

Shuman's Corner—which was named for Abraham Shuman (1839–1918), whose store was at the south corner of Washington and Summer Streets—was a thriving intersection at the turn of the twentieth century. The façade of the Jordan Marsh Company, seen on the far right, had engaged Corinthian pilasters with windows set between, which were surmounted by classical heads as keystones. Streetcars, horse-drawn delivery wagons, delivery boys and pedestrians thronged Washington Street and created a vibrant hubbub of early twentieth-century street life.

overstocks and unsold merchandise to be sold at "bargain basement sales" on an automatic markdown system. Though both basements—Filene's as well as Jordan Marsh—did quite well in selling, it was Filene's Basement that became a beloved Boston institution.

Jordan Marsh Company said:

> *Its success* [in the early twentieth century] *has been phenomenal under the generous patronage of the New England public, who found by experience that the same qualities in the lower priced merchandise, the same fair prices and the general satisfaction peculiar with the regulations between Jordan Marsh Company and its customers, existed in this unique Basement Store as it always had and always will in the "upstairs" part of the institution.*

Left: No fashionable woman in 1900 would leave home without a "Heptonette" cloak that was said to be perfect for walking, driving or traveling. The advertisement in the Jordan Marsh & Co. catalogue pledged that these cloaks were "guaranteed rain-proof, perfectly porous, odorless, no rubber" and came in three models known as Ontario, Lassie and Iris.

Right: In the days when automobiles did not have heat, Jordan Marsh & Co. offered "Gentlemen's and Chauffeurs' Fur and Fur-Lined Coats" that would keep both the driver and the passenger warm. From raccoon-lined coats, dog-skin coats and marmot-lined coats to muskrat-lined coats with an otter collar, these coats were expensive but obviously warm and showed the veritable breadth of merchandise available in the store.

The continued patronage of Bostonians of all walks of life was due, in part, to the wonderful array of merchandise that the store offered. In fact, in 1911, it was said that "Jordan Marsh Company sends more buyers to European markets than any other single store in the United States. This fact is realized by its customers, who know that this store always has a complete assortment of the finest merchandise." Eben Dyer Jordan had truly continued his and his late partner's vision into the last decade of the nineteenth century, but it was his son Eben Dyer Jordan Jr. and George W. Mitton who in the early twentieth century made Jordan Marsh Company the "Store of Famed Reliability."

Left: Trade cards were a popular way for businesses to advertise their stores in the nineteenth century. This card, with a smiling girl in a fancy costume with a feathered hat, advertised that Jordan Marsh offered not only instructions on how to play whist but also recipe books, needlework, embroidery and painting, as well as instruction for using silk, chenille and ribbon embroidery. *Courtesy of Kimberly Sliney*.

Right: The Jordan Marsh & Co. Fall 1890–Winter 1891 catalogue was published on the fortieth anniversary of the founding of the company in 1851. Depicting the various locations of the store seen on the cover, from Eben Jordan's original store on 1841 in the North End to the impressive flagship store at Washington and Avon Streets, it was a remarkable display of how the store had grown in five decades.

JORDAN MARSH TIMELINE

1840   Benjamin Lloyd Marsh starts in the North End at 168 Hanover Street. (At one time his company was known as Marsh and Bartlett and later as B.L. Marsh & Co.)

1841   Eben Dyer Jordan starts in the North End at 146 Hanover Street, corner of Mechanic Street, in a wholesale business financed by Joshua Stetson. The first customer is Miss Louisa Bareiss.

1849   Eben Jordan sells his store and becomes a salesman for James M. Bebee & Co., 88 Hanover Street, Boston's North End.

1851   Jordan and Marsh is founded on January 20 at 129 Milk Street in Boston.

1852	Charles Marsh joins the company; the store is renamed Jordan Marsh & Co.
1853	Jordan Marsh & Co. arranges European imports; Eben Dyer Jordan travels to Europe to secure funding for imports from London, Paris and Berlin.
1855	The store moves to 16, 18, 20 and 22 Pearl Street, Boston.
1857	Jordan Marsh & Co. withstands the Panic of 1857.
1859	The store moves to 148–54 Devonshire Street, between Franklin and Summer Streets, Winthrop Square, Boston, in the "Free Stone Building."
1861	Nathaniel J. Bradlee designs a store for George W. Warren (later purchased by Jordan Marsh in 1871 and located at 242–44 Washington Street).
1861	The store begins selling directly to the public.
1861	James Fisk Jr. joins the company.
1861	Any employee who enlists in the War of the Rebellion has the cost of his uniform and his salary paid while in service, and their jobs are secure upon their return. Forty-five Jordan Marsh employees enlist.
1861	George W. Mitton is hired as an errand boy; he had been employed at George W. Warren & Co. previously.
1865	Benjamin Lloyd Marsh dies.
1869	There is a Jordan Marsh office at 184–86 Church Street in New York City.
1870	Eben Dyer Jordan invests in the local newspaper the *Boston Globe*.
1870	James Clark Jordan, son of Eben Dyer Jordan, joins the company.
1871	Jordan Marsh & Co. purchases the George W. Warren & Co. business and store at 450 Washington Street in Boston; they also have 242–50 Washington Street and 14 and 16 Avon Street in Boston.
1871	The wholesale division is established.
1872	Jordan Marsh installs its first passenger elevator.
1876	Jordan Marsh installs the first store telephone, connected to the wholesale house.
1880	The clock tower building is designed by Bradlee, Winslow & Wetherall and built at the corner of Washington and Avon Streets (formerly Avon Place).
1881	Eben Dyer Jordan Jr., son of Eben Dyer Jordan, joins the company.
1882	The pneumatic tubes and cash system is installed at the store.
1886	Charles Marsh dies.

1890	Jordan Marsh reports that it has over 100,000 names on its mailing list.
1895	Eben Dyer Jordan Sr. dies.
1898	The Francis Building is built; a marble-lined pedestrian subway is built under Avon Street, connecting the Francis Building with the Main Store.
1901	There are European offices in Paris at 1 Rue Ambroise Thomas and in Berlin at 47 Ritterstrasse.
1901	The company name is changed to Jordan Marsh Company.
1902	An office is opened at 31 Union Square in New York City.
1903	There are now offices of Jordan Marsh in New York, Paris, Berlin and London.
1905	The Association for Mutual Aid is established to assist fellow employees.
1909	The Annex Building is built.
1910	Jordan Marsh Company opens a new basement store for sale of less expensive merchandise, as well as merchandise that did not sell in the departments.
1911	The Annex Building is built on the opposite side of Avon Street.
1912	Timothy J. McCarthy and Herbert H. Hilliard, buyers for Jordan Marsh, die on the sinking of the RMS *Titanic*.
1913	Edward J. Mitton dies.
1916	Eben Dyer Jordan Jr. dies.
1916	George W. Mitton becomes president of Jordan Marsh.
1919	The Quarter Century Club is established for fellow employees with twenty-five years of service.
1922	The company acquires the Abraham Shuman Company and its store at Washington and Summer Streets.
1922	The Half Century Club is established for fellow employees with fifty years of service.
1923	Jordan Marsh has an office in Kobe, Japan.
1925	The company acquires the C.H. Hovey Company and its store on Summer Street.
1926	The Beach Street Free Auto Parking Garage is built for Jordan Marsh customers driving their automobiles to town.
1929	Bristol Building, at Chauncy Street, Bedford Street and Harrison Avenue, is added to the present area, making the entire basement three blocks long.

1929   A direct entrance from Summer Street to the basement store is opened.

1929   The Santason Parade is started on Thanksgiving Day with floating balloons paraded through the city streets to signal the start of the holiday season.

1930   A new tunnel entrance to the basement store at Summer and Washington Streets is opened.

1930   Richard Mitton becomes president of Jordan Marsh.

1935   Allied Department Stores is founded, previously known as Hahn, which begins to purchase local department stores to give them larger chain store advantages.

1937   Edward Richardson Mitton becomes president of Jordan Marsh.

1943   The Santason Parade is ended due to World War II and is not resumed.

1947   Jordan Marsh takes over the C.F. Hovey Company.

1948–49 Perry, Shaw, Kehoe and Dean design a new addition for the store's upcoming centennial.

1949   Edward Richardson Mitton, president, lays the cornerstone of the new building at Summer and Chauncy Streets.

1951   Jordan Marsh celebrates the centennial of its founding.

1951   The first suburban store is opened at Shoppers World on Route 9 in Framingham, Massachusetts.

1952   Edward Richardson Mitton receives the ninth annual Tobe Award for excellence in retailing.

1954   A branch of Jordan Marsh is opened in San Diego, California, by Allied Stores.

1954   The store acquires F.N. Joslin Company in Malden.

1956   A branch of Jordan Marsh is opened in Miami, Florida, by Allied Stores.

1957   The final unit designed by Perry, Shaw, Kehoe and Dean is completed on Avon Street.

1959   The Enchanted Village of Saint Nicholas, created by the Christian Hofmann Company in West Germany, is opened and creates the mood of *Gemutlichkeit* in Boston.

1962   Edward Richardson Mitton becomes chairman of the board.

1962   Cameron S. Thompson becomes president (retires in 1966).

1966   William Payson Reed becomes president (retires in 1972).

1972   Robert Hoye becomes president (retires in 1976).

1975	Jordan Marsh store (that part formerly A. Shuman's) at Washington and Summer Streets is demolished, to the great consternation of Bostonians.
1976	William Tilburg becomes president (retired in 1982).
1982	Elliot J. Stone becomes president (retired in 1989).
1986	Allied Stores is purchased by Campeau Corporation of Montreal, Quebec.
1988	Sam L. Simmons becomes president (retired in 1989).
1988	Campeau Corporation acquires Federated Department Stores.
1989	Richard F. Van Pelt becomes president (retired in 1991).
1991	All Florida Jordan Marsh stores are disbanded and merged with Maas Brothers of Tampa, later to be absorbed by Burdines.
1991	Harold S. Frank becomes Burdines president.
1992	Former Allied Stores Corporation merges into a new company known as Federated Department Stores.
1994	Jordan Marsh is merged with Macy's, and all stores are renamed Macy's.
1995	All Jordan Marsh stores become Macy's.

The Ladies' Parlor and Waiting Room at Jordan Marsh & Co. was a "great convenience for out of-town patrons, where they can meet friends [and] have their bundles taken care of." It was comfortable, with plush carpeting and tropical plants that had desks stocked with store stationery, where one could write notes to family and friends, as well as comfortable chairs on which to rest from shopping or read a newspaper or magazine.

The Oriental Rug Parlor was located in the House Furnishing Annex. Here an elegantly dressed lady and her husband are shown imported oriental rugs that were available for their home in an exotic setting reminiscent of the Middle East.

The Soda Fountain was located in the basement of the Main Store and offered not just refreshing fountain drinks but also delicious dishes of ice cream. Jordan Marsh proclaimed that it was the largest, most progressive and most liberal store in New England, and after a day of shopping, it was pleasant to relax at the Soda Fountain. Later, this was the site of the Red Lantern Restaurant; the Spanish Tea Room was on the street floor.

The Picture Section at Jordan Marsh & Co. was located on the street floor of the House Furnishing Annex. With art shows and competitions, which were held on a regular basis, Jordan Marsh offered framed art by both well-known and emerging New England artists so one could hang original art in one's home.

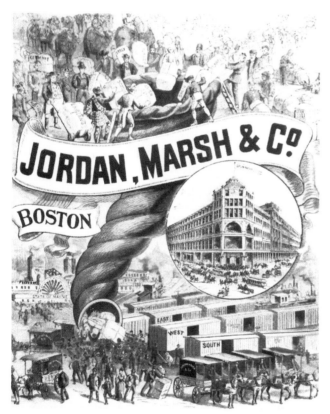

Jordan Marsh & Co. had wonderful advertising art in the late nineteenth century, with merchandise from abroad depicted as being dropped into a horn of plenty and coming out the end to be delivered by railroad, paddle boat and horse-drawn delivery wagons. "Whatever the season of the year may be, one can be sure of finding something entirely new, novel, and original at Jordan Marsh & Co."

A fanciful card from Christmas 1913 had "Christmas Greetings to the Little Folks," inviting them to visit "New England's Most Wondrous Display of Playthings," including toys, games, dolls and playthings in "a panorama that will send the childish heart into ecstasies of joy, and please the older folks as well."

E. J. Mitton

Left: Eden Dyer Jordan Jr. was made a member of the Jordan Marsh firm in 1880 upon his graduation from Harvard College. Upon the death of his father in 1895, he became president of Jordan Marsh & Co. and served as a great and innovative leader, with the assistance of George W. Mitton as vice president, until his death in 1916.

Right: Edward J. Mitton (1847–1913) started as an errand boy at Jordan Marsh in 1861 and would eventually become a vice president of the company and the progenitor of three generations of the Mitton family that oversaw the operations of Jordan Marsh Company from 1916 to 1973.

CHAPTER 3

DEPARTMENT STORE EXTRAVAGANZA

The ultimate satisfaction of customers is always held at heart.
—Jordan Marsh Company

B y the early twentieth century, Jordan Marsh, according to *Retail and Romance*, "had clothed people and shod them, furnished their houses, lighted their evenings, stocked their bookshelves, entertained their leisure with radios and talking machines, equipped them for sport, for travel, for work, for play—and provided continual thrills for bargain hunters." Eben Dyer Jordan and Benjamin Lloyd Marsh had started their dry goods store with great hopes in 1851, and by the company's diamond jubilee in 1926, it had become one of the most important and largest department stores in New England.

Benjamin Marsh had died in 1865, Charles Marsh in 1883 and Eben Jordan in 1895, but the store was to be more than ably overseen by Eben Dyer Jordan Jr. and Edward J. Mitton as president and vice president, respectively, from 1895 to the time of World War I. Throughout this period, many family members were employed by the company, among them Eben Dyer Jordan's son James Clarke Jordan and his son-in-law Herbert Dumaresq, who was married to Julia Maria Jordan. Other junior partners included James Fisk Jr., Henry W. Taylor and W.F. Watters. Edward J. Mitton's long association with Jordan Marsh began in 1861 when, as an English-born errand boy, he literally came with the recently acquired George W. Warren Store on Washington Street in Boston. Edward J. Mitton (1847–1913), working with

The Men's Daylight Clothing Section was located at the Main Store on the second floor and offered a wide array of "correct liveries for every occasion," which were available in a wide array of sizes and materials. The sheer number of salesmen seen here ensured prompt and polite service.

The Main Store stairway at Jordan Marsh was a cast-iron and steel multi-floored stairway that was modeled on the famous department store Printemps in Paris. The gentle elegance of the stairway allowed shoppers to see as well as be seen while shopping in New England's largest department store. The portrait of Eben Dyer Jordan can be seen in the center.

both Jordan father and son throughout the nineteenth century, had by 1901 become vice president of Jordan Marsh and worked closely with Eben Dyer Jordan Jr. to expand the store. Over those four decades, he rose from errand boy to silk salesman to silk buyer to head of the wholesale business, then a member of the firm and then vice president, which would begin a long association by him and his family with Jordan Marsh Company. In fact, it was commented, "For if the two Jordans have woven the warp of this great business, the Mittons have threaded its woof. And stout fabric it is, English in fiber, American in workmanship, warranted to wear forever."

The joint cooperation and ingenuity of Jordan and Mitton produced many new innovations, which were to include charge accounts, the great basement store and the well-loved Annex store for home furnishings, which was greatly expanded in 1911. Each and every new innovation was undoubtedly novel and daunting to employees, but they were soon to become the standard for growing businesses in the city. In 1876, a telephone was installed that connected the Main Store with the Wholesale House but was also available to the few customers who had them in their homes to contact the store. Glass showcases and display cabinets were installed to showcase the wide variety and style of merchandise available, as well as electric lights that illuminated the whole building day and night. Passenger elevators were installed in 1872 to replace the cumbersome stairs for the five-story building, and each elevator was operated by an employee wearing gloves who politely called out the floor and its specialties as the elevator ascended before moving the reticulated screen to allow passengers to alight. However, it was the pneumatic cash system that truly impressed customers, as the system allowed a container to be sent from the retail and wholesale sales counters to the credit department through a series of tubes for either change for a cash sale or approval for a charge to a customer's account. Each of these new-fangled things built on the reputation of Jordan Marsh as

G.W. Mitton

George W. Mitton (1869–1947) started as a stock boy at Jordan Marsh in 1887 and would eventually become president of Jordan Marsh in 1916 upon the death of Eben Dyer Jordan Jr. He served as president until 1930, when his brother Richard Mitton became president, and he assumed the position of chairman of the board.

dear to the traditions of its founders but committed to providing the best and most up-to-date store in the world.

Eben Dyer Jordan Jr. was truly his father's son. He had attended Harvard College, like his elder brother James Clark Jordan, and joined the store in 1880. He was considered an innovator, experimenter and lover of beauty. With the able assistance of Edward Mitton, he was to revolutionize his father's store. In fact as *Retail and Romance* says, "It was the idea of a department store as against the dry goods emporium dear to his father's traditions" that created the biggest change, and the result was that "Jordan's became one of New England's first department stores." Following his father's death in 1895, Eben Jr. assumed the presidency with Edward J. Mitton as vice president, assisted by W.F. Watters and George W. Mitton. The store was remade at the turn of the century and boasted of being the "Mercantile Heart of New England" in its advertisements—in essence, declaring that Jordan Marsh Company was the heart of New England. In *The Story of a Store*, this was reinforced by stating:

> *This fact is realized by its customers, who know that this store always has a complete assortment of the finest merchandise. The great function of a department store is to gather from everywhere things that are needed for life, health and comfort—concentrating them where they are wanted and arrange them for convenient selection by their customers. Also to utilize its knowledge of goods and conditions by sifting out the good from the bad, accepting only that which is trustworthy so that the most inexperienced may buy them with absolute safety. The immense institution of Jordan Marsh Company with its unlimited resources, with its unsurpassed American and European connections, with its roomy 24-acre store and its well-known reputation for absolute reliability, carries out in a superb fashion the ideal of a department store and its connection with and value to a community.*

Jordan and Mitton transformed the Main Store into a "homelike atmosphere [that] pervades everywhere," with long broad aisles lined with glass display cases, all of which were manned by the courteous and attentive salespeople who were well drilled in their respective lines. In addition to the multistory Main Store with its departments that offered handkerchiefs, laces, women's gloves and neckwear, ribbons and such were men's furnishings, shoes and hats. Jordan Marsh was to boast of twenty-four acres of floor space with forty thousand yards of carpet used to cover the floors, twenty-six passenger elevators, twelve thousand automatic fire sprinklers, one thousand

By 1910, the horse-drawn delivery wagons were being phased out, and delivery trucks were being ordered to replace them. Here, two delivery men place blanket-wrapped furniture on the truck flatbed for delivery throughout the Boston area. By 1914, the Autocar Company in Ardmore, Pennsylvania, was providing motor delivery vehicles to Jordan Marsh Company. "Their superiority under the difficulties of winter travel is particularly marked."

arc lamps, eighteen thousand incandescent lights, four miles of pneumatic tubing and a storehouse with an additional 120,000 square feet of storage space. By 1910, Jordan Marsh Company was said to receive ten thousand telephone calls daily and had over one thousand shoppers pass through its doors every day. The employees worked hard to make shopping convenient and said, "Every practical means is taken to make the shopping tour more pleasant. Two spacious, elegantly appointed Waiting Rooms, one in each building, are furnished with easy chairs, writing materials, newspapers, checkrooms, lavatories and other necessary conveniences for customers." Eben Dyer Jordan wanted to ensure that these comforts would win greater appreciation from customers and thereby they would continue to trade with the store. He also ensured customer satisfaction with a Complaint Adjustment Office, a transfer desk, the largest private branch telephone exchange in Boston with eight switchboard operators, a telegraph and cable station and even a substation of the United States Post Office, all of which were located in the Main Building. So solicitous of its customers was Jordan

Right: The Boston Town Crier boldly proclaims the Diamond Jubilee of Jordan Marsh Company in 1926. This pin was distributed to customers who shared the seventy-fifth anniversary of Jordan Marsh with justifiable pride.

Below: The 111th Birthday Sale of Jordan Marsh in 1962 had bargains galore throughout the store, as well as the early suburban stores. Here, women look at jewelry in the glass display cases in the Boston store.

Marsh Company that it even had "Special Sick-rooms," with trained nurses in attendance, that were located adjacent to the Waiting Rooms in each building for customers who were suddenly taken ill.

George W. Mitton (1869–1947,) the son of Edward J. Mitton, was to assume the presidency of Jordan Marsh after Eben Dyer Jordan Jr.'s death in 1916. He continued to maintain the store's tradition of growth and innovation, and under his leadership, the distinctions between management and workers were changed so that all employees were to be known as Jordan Marsh "Fellow Workers" going forward. He realized early on that the employees

The Jordan Marsh Great Basement Store, which was often referred to as the Bristol Building, was adjacent to the Annex on Chauncy Street between Bedford Street and Exeter Place. Here one could purchase household furnishings, upholstery and curtains, and on the second floor was the Health Department, with the company doctor, dentist and chiropodist.

The Centennial Plate (1851–1951) stated on the reverse that it "Commemorated 100 years of service to Boston and New England—A view of the new Jordan Marsh 'Store of Tomorrow' now under construction." The plate was commissioned by Jordan Marsh to be made by the Wedgwood Factory in England and showed the proposed new building designed by Perry, Shaw, Kehoe and Dean in the center, surrounded by the various earlier buildings. Other plates commissioned from Wedgwood included the Old North Church, the Old State House, Faneuil Hall, the Battle of Bunker Hill, the Battle at Concord Bridge, the Battle of the *Constitution* and the *Guerriere* and the Washington Elm.

of Jordan Marsh had longevity, and he wanted to recognize them for their continued dedication to their job and the company. He established in 1919 the Quarter Century Club, which honored twenty-five-year employees of the company, and in 1922 the Half Century Club, which had the remarkable aspect of employees with fifty years of service. In and of itself, both were commendable, but it was a high standard of working conditions, respect and liberal benefits that allowed Fellow Workers to remain in their positions.

During the vibrant economy of the 1920s, Jordan Marsh continued to expand, and in 1922, the company purchased its next-door competitor, A. Shuman & Co., which had both a ready-made and custom apparel store at the corner of Washington and Summer Streets often referred to as Shuman's Corner, to house Jordan's Store for Men. In 1925, the company acquired competitor C.F. Hovey & Co. on the same block on Summer Street. It was to remain under the Jordan Marsh name and operated as such until 1947, when the business was incorporated into the bigger store. However, though the store had bought out former competitors as early as 1861, it needed a greater leverage on purchasing power. Jordan Marsh was to become a leading unit of the Hahn Department Stores chain in 1928 and remained as such when Allied Stores succeeded it in 1935. A plan to rebuild the whole store was discussed before the Great Depression and World War II had to put it on hold. In 1935, Jordan Marsh was to be one of the founders of New York City–based Allied Stores Corporation, a successor to Hahn Department Stores, Inc. A holding company founded in 1928, Hahn brought chain store advantages to independent, family-owned department stores.

Edward R. Mitton (1896–1973) became president of Jordan Marsh in 1937 and fulfilled his father's dream of connecting the Main Store to the Annex with a three-level bridge across Avon Street. After the war, in 1947, Jordan Marsh announced that it would replace its old buildings with "the only store of its kind in the entire world" that would tower fourteen stories over Boston. Though the whole store would be new, it would carry on New England traditional architecture in its classical brick façades trimmed in limestone. Innovation took the form of continuous show windows, heated sidewalks and a stainless steel marquee to shelter shoppers from unpredictable Boston weather.

The first unit of the new store, at the corner of Summer and Chauncy Streets, was completed in October 1949, and another, along Summer Street, followed for Jordan Marsh's centennial year of 1951. The final unit to be constructed was on Avon Street and was completed in 1957. Jordan Marsh's suburban growth, and the subsequent stagnation in downtown Boston retail

The Jordan Marsh store at Shoppers World opened in 1951 and had the great claim to fame that its roof was the third-largest dome in the world. The Jordan Marsh "Observer" invited the public to "Come marvel at the gigantic, wonderfully-lighted acres of beautifully displayed merchandise…for your home, your family and yourself!" As the first suburban store, it would eventually be part of a network of stores that were opened throughout New England and in New York, California and Florida.

Jordan Marsh Company, in 1935, showed the newest and most fashionable "Vogue Patterns" for the stylish woman of the day. Many female customers looked to Jordan Marsh, which became an arbiter of fashion in the twentieth century.

Jordan Marsh became known for providing wedding dresses for "World War II War Brides" at a moment's notice. Seen here in 1943, this chic two-piece dress "designed for travel" and veiled straw hat were worn at a wedding that had a short furlough honeymoon. The groom doesn't look too bad either in his regulation navy whites.

Kasper for Joan Leslie zeroes in on the big zip . . . now on a casual jersey coat, belted over its own striped shift, 160.00. Jordan Marsh Designers' Shop.

Above, left: Jordan Marsh was a style arbiter, as seen here in this very elegant black dress that was designed by Christian Dior and available in the store.

Above, right: A fashion show in 1972 had a model walking the runway in the Jordan Marsh Annex, as ladies in the audience seem to cringe at the new fashion trend of dresses being hemmed above the knee.

Left: Jordan Marsh Designers' Shop offered Kasper for Joan Leslie. A fishnet-clad model wears a casual jersey coat belted over its own striped shift with a felt hat as she poses in front of the meetinghouse at Old Sturbridge Village in Sturbridge, Massachusetts.

sales, put an end to Edward Mitton's dream of a completely new Jordan Marsh store, and what was built was reduced in size and scope. The store operated until 1975 as a conglomeration of old and new structures cobbled together: the old Main Store on the corner of Washington Street and Avon Street, the New Store at Summer and Chauncy Streets, the Store for Men at Washington and Summer Streets, the Annex across from the Main Store and the Bristol Building that housed the budget store home furnishings division on its first floor.

In May 1975, Allied Stores, with the full sanction of the Boston Redevelopment Authority, demolished all of the old Jordan Marsh buildings and expanded the newer portions with a bland brick box that would replace the old "Shuman's Corner." Devoid of the well-loved Annex, a consolidated and remodeled Jordan Marsh would be connected to a new multi-use facility along Washington Street known as Lafayette Place. In 1996, the end had come when all Jordan Marsh stores in the northeastern United States, already part of the Macy's East division, were converted to the Macy's nameplate.

The new addition to Jordan Marsh had light that was projected through aluminum gratings, known as flexible modules, which allowed workmen to access the electrical wiring above. The effect was to be bright light in the store interior, as seen here in men's dress shirts, even on the darkest days.

A trio of young salesmen tallies their daily sales in the men's dress shirt department. These illuminated glass display cases held a wide selection of shirts in various colors, materials and neck sizes and were popular with shoppers.

Customers inspect telescopes in the Scientific and Construction Department at Jordan Marsh in 1965. These telescopes allowed people to study the heavens with magnification lenses that offered glimpses into the universe, all from the comfort of their own home.

Left: A salesman hawks to shoppers "The Original Gyroscope," which was entertaining and educational as well as loads of fun for everyone in the family. Everyone seemed to want one, as it had been "Seen on television…Rex Trailer's Show" and became the toy of the day, as it was "loads of fun for young and old."

Below: A salesman gathers a group of shoppers and their children for an impromptu magic show at his counter that was not only entertaining but also created great curiosity as to how that trick was exactly done. The "Do It Yourself Magic Show" was available from Jordan Marsh for you to perform the tricks at home to entertain family and friends.

During the holiday season, the displays and decorations were incredible, and each department was staffed by salesmen and women intent on explaining every aspect of the merchandise. With throngs of shoppers, holiday music being played and festive holiday decorations, it was undoubtedly a mounting crescendo up to Christmas Eve.

This salesman is the center of attention as children gather around his station as he uses a deck of cards for a series of mechanical tricks that state "no skill required." These card games were fun, and Jordan Marsh Company's Toyland was a major destination of New England youth.

Dollar Day at Jordan Marsh was usually the first Wednesday of the month. A blue Jordan Marsh dollar bill would be issued to customers that was "good for one dollar in merchandise at all our stores." These bargains were eagerly looked forward to by frugal customers, as one never knew what merchandise would be available.

CHAPTER 4

FRIENDLY COMPETITORS IN BOSTON

A satisfied customer is your best advertisement....Satisfy her at any cost.
She is the boss.
—Eben Dyer Jordan Jr.

Although Jordan Marsh is considered the first real "department store" in Boston, with numerous distinct departments eventually under five roofs that had many acres of display space, there were many other well-known and well-patronized stores in Boston, each of which was unique and had its own loyal clientele. The downtown shopping area was fondly known at the turn of the twentieth century as Shuman's Corner in honor of Abraham Shuman, whose department store was at the corner of Summer and Washington Streets before being bought in 1922 by Jordan Marsh and incorporated into the Main Store. Located along the major streets in the downtown area—Summer, Washington, Winter and Tremont Streets—were at least a dozen well-known department stores that had loyal followings and were considered to be the friendly competitors of Jordan Marsh.

A. SHUMAN'S

Abraham Shuman's Department Store was located at the corner of Washington and Summer Streets. Abraham Shuman (1839–1918) was a

Looking west on Summer Street toward Shuman's Corner, the junction of Summer, Washington and Winter Streets was completely built up by the turn of the twentieth century with department stores, specialty shops and small stores. The spire of the Park Street Church on Tremont Street can be seen in the distance.

very successful retail clothing merchant in Boston. Having emigrated from Prussia with his family in 1848, he opened his business a decade later at the corner of Washington and Vernon Streets in Roxbury, Massachusetts, and within a few years, he was joined in partnership by John Phillips under the firm name of Phillips and Shuman, later to be renamed A. Shuman & Co. of Boston. The store was considered the pioneer firm in the United States in the manufacture and wholesaling of boys' and men's clothing. The success of his expanded business would lead to Shuman becoming referred to as "the wealthiest clothing manufacturer and retailer in Boston in the nineteenth century." His landmark store gave the name "Shuman's Corner" to the intersection of Washington, Summer and Winter Streets in the late nineteenth century; today, it is referred to as Downtown Crossing.

LEOPOLD MORSE

Leopold Morse (originally Maas) (1831–1892) was born in Wachenheim, Rhenish Palatinate, Bavaria, and came to Boston in 1849. He began his rise to fame and fortune as an errand boy for a dry goods store on Milk Street in Boston but was soon working for Henry Herman, a clothing dealer who encouraged Morse to open his own clothing store, which he eventually did but well south of the city in New Bedford, Massachusetts. Eventually, the business prospered to such a point that he purchased Herman's business and reopened it as Leopold Morse & Co. on Brattle Street in the Old West End of Boston, now the site of Boston City Hall. It was said, undoubtedly justly, that "in business he was one of the conspicuous successes of New England, and his great wealth was generously used."

Leopold Morse built a substantial five-story white marble façade store at the corner of Washington and Brattle Streets, near Scollay Square, and became one of the largest retailers of ready-made suits, which was a burgeoning business in the mid-nineteenth century. Among his business competitors were A. Shuman & Co., Kennedy's, Raymond's and Jordan Marsh Department Stores, all of which provided ready-made clothing that only needed slight tailoring. Through his business efforts, Morse became a wealthy man and was so well respected in Boston that in 1876 he was elected to the United States Congress, where "he attracted attention by his independent course in legislation." It was said that during "Mr. Morse's congressional career of 10 years, he was most useful to his constituents, and was especially the friend of all sorts of people in their dealings with the government."

Prominent in many charities in Boston, he was to found and endow the Boston Home for Aged and Infirm Hebrews and Orphanage. Opened in 1889, the Morse Home was in the former Cornell-Austin House that stood on Mattapan Street (now Blue Hills Parkway) between Eliot Street and Brook Road in Milton, just south of Mattapan Square. The impressive Greek Revival mansion was remodeled to provide thirty-two rooms and had a sixty-bed capacity for elderly and orphaned Hebrews. The credo of the Leopold Morse Home was: "Make each person young and old feel that they are our guests and are to be treated accordingly." This home was a necessary one, as most in the Boston area excluded Jews, and he truly extolled the virtue of a kindhearted and benevolent man. Thanks to his generosity, which the Morse family continued after his death, the Leopold Morse Home was fully occupied until it was closed in 1914 when a larger facility was built in Dorchester due to a sharply increased need.

Houghton and Dutton

In 1859, Benjamin Franklin Dutton (1831–1915) came to Boston and engaged in the small ware and millinery jobbing business under the firm name of B.F. Dutton & Co. In the firm of B.F. Dutton & Co., Dutton's partner was John B. Smith, who would later serve as governor of New Hampshire. In 1874, Dutton's connection with the present house of Houghton and Dutton began when a partnership with S.S. Houghton was started under the firm name that is so well known throughout New England. The department store of Houghton and Dutton is said to have been one of the largest and most popular stores in Boston.

Houghton and Dutton was a ten-story department store located for over fifty years in the Albion Building at the corner of Tremont and Beacon Streets. The store grew, had additions built and, at its peak, had most of the Albion Building leased as further retail space. After the death of Houghton, his interests were bought by Harry Dutton, who was to become the head

Well-dressed shoppers throng Shuman's Corner, what was to become known as Downtown Crossing, at Washington, Summer and Winter Streets in 1935.

of the firm and in control of the enormous business of the concern. A great following developed, and the company was successfully led for most of its life by Harry Dutton, a nephew of Benjamin Franklin Dutton, who served as president. Sadly, this well-respected Boston store fell on hard times in the 1930s following the Great Depression, as did so many department stores. The store was closed by 1935, and the building was leased to various companies until 1967, when it was demolished to build One Beacon Street, a luxury high-rise office building.

C.F. HOVEY & CO.

In 1841, Charles Fox Hovey (1807–1859) joined Washington Williams and James H. Bryden as partners in C.F. Hovey & Co. The partners were importers and wholesale dealers in dry goods, with an office at 65 Water Street in Boston. Hovey developed an interest in the retail side of the business, and in 1846, Hovey, Williams & Co. were joined by Richard C. Greenleaf and John Chandler, who already owned a retail dry goods store on Washington Street. The new company moved to 13 Winter Street, the first commercial firm to locate in the area, and eventually opened their store on Summer Street between Chauncy and Washington Streets, where they remained for a century.

C.F. Hovey & Co. was to become an innovator in department store merchandising. Plainly marked goods with a one-price system, the adoption of early closing hours, profit-sharing for employees and a credit system, utilizing monthly bills, were just some of the now-standard practices that were introduced by Hovey's. In addition to the store in Boston, the company maintained offices in New York and Paris.

After Hovey's death in 1859, the store continued to bear his name. C.F. Hovey & Co. was noted for the high quality of its merchandise, as well as for the incredible longevity of its management and partners. William Endicott Jr., Henry Woods and Samuel Johnson became partners in 1851. Woods and Johnson would remain with Hovey's until their respective deaths in 1902 and 1899; Endicott retired in 1910 after a remarkable sixty-four years in the business. Jordan Marsh bought the company in 1925, and though it retained the Hovey name until 1947, the building was demolished the next year to make way for the new Jordan Marsh Company addition designed by Perry, Shaw, Kehoe and Dean and built for the upcoming centennial of Jordan Marsh.

Gilchrist's

Gilchrist's was one of the major Boston department stores in downtown Boston a century ago and was located at the corner of Washington and Winter Streets, just across from both Filene's and Jordan Marsh. These three stores created a sort of triumvirate of early twentieth-century Boston shopping.

Gilchrist's was established in 1842 by George Turnbull, but by the late nineteenth century, Robert and John Gilchrist had become owners and continued to expand the store so that, by the end of the nineteenth century, it was necessary to see a major expansion. The new Gilchrist's Department Store was designed by the noted architect R. Clipston Sturgis and built in 1899, and though not considered as high-end as its neighbors, it was a popular and successful store that grew tremendously over the next few decades. As a department store, it offered "cloaks, capes, silks, French goods,

The former A. Shuman Company building was bought by Jordan Marsh in 1922 and incorporated into Jordan Marsh, making it an entire city block. The elegant bronze and glass canopy offered shelter to customers entering the store on the Summer Street side, flanked by display windows showing the latest fashions.

flowers, feathers, etc., [and] was a marvel to behold," but it was justly famous for its delicious macaroons, which became a store specialty in the twentieth century. The first floor of the store was said in a newspaper article to be "flooded with sunlight. So is every one of the five floors for that matter. The rays, unobstructed, shoot in from the front, which is all glass, from the rear, which has many windows, and down from above through a well, which descends from the roof clear to the ground apartment. No electric lamps are lighted in the daytime." The *Boston Globe* described the store four years after the new high-rise opened: "On the first floor the wide aisles are arched with twining morning glories and graceful sweeps of roses, while everywhere on the counters spring time is suggested by the profusion of palms. Hundreds of golden cages in which canary birds sing cheerfully all day long, are suspended from the ceilings."

In the 1940s, Gilchrist's started to branch out, and by 1964, the store had eight locations throughout Massachusetts: Quincy, Brockton, Framingham, Medford, Waltham, Stoneham, Cambridge and Dorchester. The company's store in Cambridge was located in the basement of the Star Market grocery store at the Porter Square shopping center. With the ascendancy of the automobile after World War II and the spread of shopping malls throughout the suburbs of Boston, the triumvirate declined and saw less foot traffic over the next three decades. Gilchrist's continued until its eventual closing in 1977. Its Downtown Crossing store was replaced with a shopping mall called The Corner in the original building, with offices in the upper stories.

FILENE'S

William Filene (1830–1901), a German Jew from Posen, Prussia, who immigrated to the United States in 1848 after abandoning law school in Berlin, opened in 1851 a store on Hanover Street in Boston's North End. Edward Albert and Abraham Lincoln Filene, his sons, were to become two of the most well-known businessmen in America in the early twentieth century and were responsible for turning their father's clothing store into one of the largest department stores in the country, known as the William Filene's Sons Company, the "World's Largest Specialty Store." The two sons, innovators in merchandising techniques and employer-employee relations, assumed management of the store in 1891 and inherited the store upon their father's death in 1901. They would establish minimum-wage scales for female employees, employee welfare plans, paid winter vacations for employees, employee purchasing discounts, profit sharing, health clinics, insurance programs and credit unions.

In 1909, Edward Filene established the Automatic Bargain Basement, whereby unsold merchandise moved from the floor to the basement as prices were gradually reduced on a set schedule that was prominently displayed on the wall. Edward Filene's influence gave the store an early reputation as a customer-oriented store with slogans like "money back if not satisfied." As goods remained unsold, they were eventually donated to charity. Though the bargain basement did not make a profit for many years, it attracted loyal customers and eventually turned a profit, even supporting the main store of Filene's during the Great Depression. Filene's was designed by Chicago architect Daniel Burnham and built in 1912 at the corner of Washington and Summer Streets. By 1929, Filene's had grown tremendously and would expand its operation by converting the block around Washington, Summer, Hawley and Franklin Streets into one large department store.

In 1928, Edward Filene was ignobly ousted from store management by his fellow stockholders, who were said to be concerned over his liberal management policies, but he was ironically allowed to retain the title of president. Filene's was owned by Federated Department Stores from 1929 until 1988, at which time it was acquired by the May Department Stores Company from 1988 to 2005. In 2006, the store was acquired by Macy's.

FILENE'S BASEMENT

The history of Filene's Basement is a fascinating example of how one could successfully market and sell surplus or discontinued merchandise from a major department store in a posted automatic markdown policy. Filene's Department Store was to become a beloved and well-known landmark in Boston at the corner of Summer and Washington Streets. In 1908, Edward A. Filene—son of William Filene, the founder of Filene's—came up with the idea of selling the surplus and overstocked merchandise in the basement of the department store. Thus, Filene's Automatic Bargain Basement, as it was originally called, opened for business in 1909.

As one report said:

Looking north on Washington Street in 1967, the "Downtown Crossing," as the area had become unofficially known, was still a thriving shopping area, but it had been affected by shopping malls that catered to those living in suburbia after World War II.

The Automatic Markdown system was compelling enough to lure shoppers of all different classes to the Basement, where everyone was treated equally in their efforts to shop for deals. Many shoppers would play hiding games, pushing desired items that were scheduled for further markdowns between other items, with the intention of returning to the store later to purchase them at their new, lower price. It was all about the thrill of the find.

It was a game for some, as often luxury merchandise was offered at drastically reduced prices over a period of weeks.

A great attraction for thrifty shoppers of the twentieth century, Filene's Basement tried to expand, but this led to the temporary bankruptcy of the chain. Retail Ventures Inc. bought the company in 2000. In 2006, Macy's bought the Filene's brand and closed its Downtown Crossing location, along with the historic and nationally famous basement below. Sadly, the Automatic Bargain Basement, so beloved by savvy Bostonians and tourists, closed and is now a part of "Lost Boston."

KENNEDY'S

Kennedy's Department Store was opened in 1892 at the corner of Hyde Park Avenue and River Street in Cleary Square, Hyde Park. Founded by Frederick J. Kennedy, the store specialized in men's suits and accessories and would offer to refund the nickel streetcar fare to anyone who came to the department store and made a purchase. Kennedy's was to become so successful that it moved in 1912 to a store at the corner of Summer and Hawley Streets in downtown Boston and went on to become a Boston landmark for men's suits. An early slogan was "Kennedy's: Boston's Largest, Liveliest, Leading Men's Store." Kennedy's renovated all five floors of the building and during the 1930s occupied the rest of the ground floor as well as opening a women's department on its third floor to keep up with all the stiff competition that was coming from friendly competitors. In 1937, a girls' department was also opened and was to make Kennedy's a clothing and accessories store for the entire family, though it still specialized in men's suits and accessories. By 1977, Kennedy's had been bought by Van Heusen Corporation and was later merged with Hamburger and Sons of Baltimore before closing in 1992.

E. T. SLATTERY COMPANY

E.T. Slattery Company was founded by Ellen T. Slattery in 1867. She had begun her modest but fashionable women's clothing shop on Hayward Place, but after a series of moves, the store was located in 1901 at 156 Tremont Street, overlooking the Boston Common. By the 1930s, Slattery's had grown to such proportions that the store took up three entire adjoining buildings and offered fashionable women's clothing, furs and distinctive accessories, in addition to children's clothing and a small assortment of men's furnishings.

Slattery's was one of the early Boston-based stores that began to look to the nearby suburbs to further serve their loyal shoppers who wanted to shop locally; many wealthy Bostonians had started moving to the suburbs, and the store realized that branch stores would ultimately prove successful. Slattery's opened its first branch store in Wellesley in 1920 and shortly thereafter, in 1927, in Brookline, which was well located, as the store was on the ground floor of Coolidge Corner's new Pelham Hall. One of the more unusual annual traditions of the store was the "Ball and Chain Club," which sought

In an advertisement from 1946 saluting the centennial of the *Boston Herald*, a leading city newspaper, Jordan Marsh offered "esteem for so proud an anniversary as a hundredth" and proclaimed its store as the "Mercantile Heart of New England."

new and recurring members at Christmastime each year to help "solve men's gift problems" for gentlemen who just needed some extra guidance in shopping for that perfect gift for their wives, daughters and lady friends.

Though the suburban branches of the store had done quite well, times were changing, and the Brookline store was closed just after World War II, leaving the once elegant space to become a foreign car dealership for the next several decades. Slattery's directed its efforts and focus on the Boston location and the Wellesley branch for the next few years until the store was closed due to bankruptcy in 1957. Ironically, Filene's came to the bankruptcy auction and bought all the remaining stock to sell off in its famous bargain basement.

R.H. STEARNS

Richard Hall Stearns (1824–1909) was a successful store magnate, philanthropist and politician whose self-titled department store became one of the largest chains in Boston and the surrounding suburbs. The headquarters and main store was in the impressive R.H. Stearns Building on Tremont Street opposite the Boston Common. In 1846, Stearns moved to Boston and worked in the store of C.C. Burr. A year later, Stearns opened up his own business in a small shop that later grew into a large store and company, R.H. Stearns & Co.

R.H. Stearns & Co. became a fixture in the downtown Boston shopping scene for over a century and also opened a few branch stores in the Greater Boston area. The store catered to the "carriage trade," a term used for well-to-do customers, and was particularly noted for its women's clothing, the "stereotypical Stearns customer being a white-gloved older woman of subdued upper-crust demeanor, although well-crafted children's items were also sold, as well as men's clothing, silver and crystal—but not appliances." In the early 1920s, R.H. Stearns & Co. was bought by James Nelson and Bob Maynard. In the mid-twentieth century, Carl N. Schmalz (1898–1979), son of a general store owner in Huntley, Illinois, served as president and later board chairman; Schmalz arranged the sale of the company to Edward Goodman, former president of Abraham and Straus, in 1975, after which the business closed in 1978.

By the mid-1970s, the changing face of the retail marketplace caught up with the store, and it did not have the financial backing like Filene's or Jordan Marsh, which were both owned by large national retail holding companies. At the time of Stearns's demise, Filene's was owned by Federated Department Stores and Jordan Marsh was owned by Allied Stores. R.H. Stearns was able to operate through the Christmas shopping season of 1977 but was closed in January 1978 after holding a liquidation sale.

Boston lost one of its grand stores—the last really old-style Boston store that was left—and with it died the vision of the "little old lady from Beacon Hill."

R.H. WHITE

R.H. White's was a leader in the Boston retail scene and had a very loyal following. Founded in 1853 by Ralph H. White, the store's first place of business was on Winter Street but moved to its own store designed by Peabody and Stearns in 1876. It was a highly admired building designed between 518 and 536 Washington Street. The store was previewed to an admiring public just after Christmas, on December 27, 1876. This block-long building would house the main branch of the R.H. White Company for the rest of its Boston existence.

Filene's bought the store in 1928, retaining the R.H. White name, and then in 1944, City Stores took over. City Stores may have mismanaged it a bit, and that led to a decline. The tired but stunning building sat vacant at first. Filene's used the street floor for a Christmas warehouse event in the Christmas season of 1957, but City Stores tried to use the location for Citymart. This venture used some of the floors and lasted for part of the early '60s, and then it, too, failed to interest the public. The area south of Avon Street was changing, and that part of Washington Street was looking a bit downtrodden and not very appealing to the average shopper.

The store was given a makeover of sorts both in and out. The old electric sign with a clock on Washington Street was removed and soon replaced with a more modern-looking store signature sign. The outer lower walls were given a brick-over in white, and the store boasted of wider aisles, escalators from the first to sixth floors and bright fluorescent lighting on every sales floor. R.H. White's was old in Boston retailing tradition but modern and ready for the changing marketplace of the 1950s.

A Patriot's Day Parade was held in honor of the store's 100th year, and many store window displays were featured throughout the year as a way

In 1952, Mademoiselle Rosane Brussaux came to Jordan Marsh, where she set up window displays that carried the story of the development of the romantic perfume industry in eight authentic tableaux. She is seen in front of one of her tableaux with bottles of her famous Vera Violetta perfume on either side. Roger et Gallet was one of the major French perfumers that was founded by merchant Charles Armand Roger and banker Charles Martial Gallet in 1862.

of marking this very special occasion. The most famous window display of the year was done in February 1953 and re-created the various shops of 1853 Boston all along the Washington Street side of the store. Each window became a shop of old and had frames built outside that looked as if the store was sitting right in front of the viewer. The new "W" logo was introduced this year and replaced the standard logo that had been in use for many years. The new "W" logo was also introduced into the popular Christmas slogan, "Make It a White Christmas!"

In 1953, no hint of what was to come in 1957 was in the air. R.H. White's was moving ahead, and the Boston store was its flagship and its main focus. White's management was very vocal during these early years of the 1950s about wanting to limit traffic in downtown Boston and encouraging patrons to use the public transport systems to shop rather the family car. However, even White's would bend a bit by vacating a warehouse building it used nearby so that it could be razed for a public parking garage, which was hoped would save downtown Boston from losing the loyal customers.

R.H. White's was trying desperately to keep patrons walking from the center of downtown shopping to its end of Washington Street, and the use of its store windows as a "lure" became crucial for survival. The 1953 anniversary did result in many onlookers who stopped in to shop. For the next few years, White's would carry on until it was closed in 1957.

CONRAD AND CHANDLER

Conrad and Chandler was the result of the merging of two smaller department stores in 1958. Conrad's was located on Winter Street and Chandler & Co. was on Tremont Street, and each store had a strong client base and had long histories dating well back into the nineteenth century. Both stores grew larger and added on departments such as infant and toddler goods, a small selection of men's apparel, beauty salons and some children's toys and clothing. A woman could have her complete wardrobe provided by either shop and also do a great deal of her family Christmas shopping there with ease.

Conrad's became known as "that distinctive store on Winter Street," a slogan that would be carried into the merger in 1958. Both stores had impressive buildings, but Chandler's on the corner of Tremont and West Street was by far the larger of the two. It had eleven floors, and its location facing Boston Common put it in the class of R.H. Stearns and C. Crawford Hollidge's stores. History and accessibility made both stores survivors of the Boston retail scene, and by the 1950s, Chandler's had a branch store in Belmont, proving financial viability. The store was not the magnet for shoppers that it used to be, as shopping in Boston had been superseded by suburban shopping malls. Conrad and Chandler continued to decline until 1970, when it was closed.

C. CRAWFORD HOLLIDGE

C. Crawford Hollidge was an upscale women's clothing store in Boston with clothing that displayed a distinctive style in the early twentieth century. Started by Clarence Crawford Hollidge (1878–1939), it was renowned for its red-carpet customer service and the fact that, with a prearranged appointment, one could have a personal shopper who would select items for a customer and help with fittings, as well as accessories and jewelry.

The department store was on the corner of Tremont Street and Temple Place, facing the Boston Common, and had branch stores in the upscale suburban communities of Hyannis, Wellesley and Cohasset. The store would become a rival of R.H. Stearns Department Store, which was located on the opposite corner. A disastrous fire destroyed the business in 1967, and it was closed.

RAYMOND'S

Raymond's Department Store was opened in 1872 by George J. Raymond (1852–1915) and was located at the corner of Washington and Franklin Streets, opposite Bromfield Street. The store had the venerable Yankees Unkle Eph and Aunt Abby (often misspelled) as its well-known spokespersons, which created one of the more outlandish and unique of all the Boston stores. Raymond's also was quite adept at getting publicity, including when thousands of people would line the streets of Boston when the circus came to town to watch the elephants arriving by train and then paraded through the streets—with placards sponsored by Raymond's. A local newspaper reported the following:

In 1949, Jordan Marsh had a competition held in conjunction with the showing of the movie *The Secret Garden*, a screen adaptation of the classic 1911 novel by Frances Hodgson Burnett. The person selecting the key (in reference to the key to the Secret Garden) to the Astor Theater from a barrel holding thirty-five thousand keys at the Jordan Marsh Garden Shop would win this seventy-three-piece chest of silver flatware and a silver tea and coffee service. Jordan Marsh display manager Walter Krysto and American Airline stewardess Constance Conlan admire the silver.

Raymond's department store was a fixture in downtown Boston for 100 years. Its spokesman was "Unkle Eph," a bewhiskered top-hatted swamp Yankee with an eye for a bargain and a problem with spelling. Every year, with much fanfare [and advance publicity,] *"Unkle Eph" arrived at South Station and was led to the store by a marching band to celebrate "originashun day," the anniversary of the opening of the store.*

So much popular interest was created in Unkle Eph, Aunt Abby and their village friends that in 1926, Frank Dorr, then president of Raymond's, decided to have them visit the store in person and hold a gigantic sale while they were there. This first Unkle Eph Day was such a wild success that it became a semi-annual event until 1942.

Raymond's posted its credo in a letter to its customers called "Only A Store":

Where all the people can buy merchandise, that's all. Merely a store, not a lottery, BUT A STORE, the results of years of hard work catering to the interests of the people. NO STAMPS, no tinsel shows, no catchpenny schemes of any nature, NO BAD CHARGE ACCOUNTS (for you to pay for), NO FANCY FIXTURES, NO Expensive Delivery Systems, no P.M.'s to clerks to force you to buy unusable merchandise, no Turn-over men so you can't get out with a whole suit if you don't buy, no Fancy Expressions, no Hired Brains to write mushy, slushy advertising, no High Salaried Wallflowers—NOTHING TO PAY FOR BUT THE GOODS YOU BUY—on the Express Condition that YOU'RE THE BOSS and MUST be satisfied or Get Your Money Back quickernlitenin.

Yours truly,

RAYMOND'S

Raymond's also operated suburban stores in Dedham, Lynn, Malden, Quincy and Waltham. The store filed for bankruptcy in 1972 and closed shortly thereafter.

SIEGEL'S

Siegel's Department Store was located in an impressive building designed by Arthur H. Bowditch and built in 1905 at the corner of Washington and Essex Streets. Promising one-stop shopping, Siegel's was said to offer everything under one roof, which included a ladies' writing and reception room, photo studio, delicatessen, bakery, post office and telegraph office, bank and restaurant that could seat one thousand diners at a time. The department store was to last only two decades before it closed, and the Keith-Albee Boston Theater opened on the first floor of the building in 1925.

Within the large Siegel building was an office complex and a theater with three thousand seats that was designed by Thomas Lamb. The Keith-Albee Boston Theater, later to be known as WRKO-Boston (for "Radio-Keith-Orpheum"), was located here and proved to be not just a popular movie theater but also where Arlene Francis and Bob Chester and his orchestra hosted the immensely popular *Blind Date* radio show. This radio program was broadcast throughout the New England area and was immensely popular

Jordan Marsh sponsored an Irish-themed week in March 1968 that included the Bunratty Singers from Ireland. Seen, *left to right*, are S.A. Carroll, governor of the Bank of Ireland; Robert G. Hoye, vice president of Jordan Marsh; Colm Barnes, chairman of Irish Export Board; George Colley, Irish minister of industry and commerce; William P. Reed, president of Jordan Marsh; William P. Fay, ambassador to Ireland; and Gearoid O'Clerigh, Irish consul general in Boston.

for many years through 1945. Afterward, the theater became known as the Essex, an adult entertainment movie house.

Today, the building is referred to as the Washington-Essex Building and has been remodeled for offices of the Commonwealth of Massachusetts.

THE SHEPARD STORES

The Shepard Stores in Boston, which also had a store in Providence, Rhode Island, was located on Tremont Street just south of Winter Street adjacent to St. Paul's Episcopal Cathedral, conveniently located for shoppers opposite the kiosk of the Park Street Station. The store also had entrances on Winter Street and Tremont Place and was a popular and well-patronized store that was founded by John Shepard Sr. The store was originally known as the Shepard Norwell & Co. and dated back to 1865. The department store was operated by three generations of the Shepard family as a veritable "store of 'stores'....The Shepard idea was to treat each department like a small specialty shop within the larger parent store." The name of the department store was eventually changed to the Shepard Stores following World War I.

John Shepard III, the grandson of the founder, was also a successful radio entrepreneur, and the Boston store was to become the location of a radio venture beginning in 1922 known as WNAC Radio (today WRKO). He was one of the original board members of the National Association of Broadcasters, having been elected the group's first vice president in 1923, and his New England radio network was known as the Yankee Network. His father, John Shepard Jr., made the decision in 1937 that he was too old to continue to operate the store and noted that his son was mainly involved with his radio properties. The Boston store was closed, but the Providence Shepard store remained open, with Robert Shepard continuing its operation. It was said that Filene's Basement purchased all of the remaining stock and sold it in its basement store during the early months of 1938.

CHAPTER 5

EXPANSION DOWNTOWN
TO THE SUBURBS

The spirit of the organization is what counts most.

JORDAN 🚢 MARSH

Jordan Marsh was to see extensive expansion from the Downtown Boston Flagship Store to the suburbs following World War II; the following are branch stores and the years they were opened.

1951 Shoppers World, Framingham, MA
1954 San Diego, CA (closed in 1958)
1954 Malen Square, Malden, MA
1956 Miami, FL (followed by multiple stores in Florida)
1958 North Shore Shopping Mall, Peabody, MA
1966 Bedford, NH
1967 South Shore Shopping Mall, Braintree, MA
1968 Burlington Mall, Burlington, MA
1969 Maine Mall, Portland, ME
1970 Warwick Mall, Warwick, RI
1971 Worcester Center Galleria, Worcester, MA
1972 Squantum Warehouse, Quincy, MA

1975 Lowell, MA
1977 Methuen Mall, Methuen, MA
1978 Brockton, MA
1978 Cape Cod Mall, Hyannis, MA
1988 Swansea, MA
1991 All Florida stores are disbanded, merged with Maas Brothers
1994 Natick Mall, Natick, MA
1995 All stores become Macy's

In the period just after the Great Depression, Richard Mitton, the son of George W. Mitton, became president of Jordan Marsh Company in 1930. Great changes were taking place, as it was in 1935 that Allied Department Stores (previously known as Hahn) was founded and began to purchase local department stores in the United States to give them larger chain store advantages. As a result, Jordan Marsh, which joined Allied, had an edge of the purchasing power of a larger entity, which allowed it to offer quality merchandise at somewhat reduced cost.

The fanciful automated figures on the Jordan Marsh Circus were made by Hans Christian Hofmann in West Germany and attracted children from throughout New England to visit Jordan Marsh. Though there were no live animals, these automated animals and figures entertained throngs of visitors.

An automated figure of a bear riding a unicycle and holding flags in both hands would circle the circus display as the uniformed bear trainer moved in unison.

Jordan Marsh was also a large entity that had numerous stores—the Main Store, including the Annex; the Men's Store (formerly A. Shuman Store) at the corner of Washington and Summer Streets; Hovey's on Summer Street; and the Great Basement Store. The store had grown tremendously since the early twentieth century and also had off-site locations such as a warehouse at the army base in South Boston that had "eight floors of warehouse and workrooms employing a hundred and ninety-three people in the manufacture of bedding and furniture, in furniture upholstering and finishing, in the making of window shades, carpets, sofa pillows and in all kinds of repairing." Jordan Marsh also offered custom shirts for gentlemen and employed over fifty workers just in men's and boys' clothing manufacturing. The store continued to offer such luxuries as the Dressmaking Salon, which was on the sixth floor of the Main Building in an exquisitely decorated salon that was "paneled in ivory, velvet floored, hung with mauve ceiling silk, softly lighted and silent, with a brilliant, parading model or two to bespeak Paris." This salon was created by Margaret Leonie Mitton, wife of the president, and took its place among the more haute couture dress shops in Boston. It was known for "its original costume designing." Also during this time was opened within the Annex the Antique Shop and Collector's Gallery with its "Little Colonial House" that had real mullioned windows, hardwood floors and colonial framework, which created an appropriate backdrop to the antiques, both authentic as well as newly made in the "antique style," that were offered to the affluent shoppers who sought something unique with which to accent their homes. These specialty shops, be they custom gentlemen's shirts, imported couture from Europe, antiques, silver or chinaware and crystal, ensured that the department store offered the very best to its customers.

One of the interesting competitions that Richard Mitton sponsored at this time was covered in the *Boston Globe* as well as the *Boston Evening Transcript* on July 2, 1935. It was a competition with New England–based architects who submitted designs for houses for the up-and-coming middle class with model one-family houses in the Jordan Marsh "Home Development Plan." There were four classes of houses, with the overall cost of the houses increasing from Class A to Class D. Over three hundred architects submitted floor plans and elevations of their house designs, seven of which were to be built throughout the Boston area, in East Milton, West Roxbury, Newton, Wellesley, Belmont, Winchester and Melrose, in cooperation with the Federal Housing Administration. Among the architects who submitted twelve drawings was Robert L. Stevenson, who won Classes A and D, as well as a second prize and three honorable mentions. Stevenson had an architectural office at 101 Tremont Street established in 1920, where he specialized in residential architecture. A graduate of the Rhode Island School of Design as well as the Beaux Arts School in New York, his early architectural training was with Stanford White of New York.

Wendell R. Holt won Class B and Raymond J. Percival won Class C; each of these winners received $500. The architects also included Royal Barry Wills, Charles F. Goodale, C. Pliny Currier, Israel Nigrosh, Constantin A. Pertzoff and J. Williams Beal, all of whom were recognized as either having been awarded the second prize or honorable mention, which brought $250 and $75, respectively. The judges of the competition were Richard Bellows, FAIA, chairman of the Boston Municipal Art Commission; William Emerson, FAIA, dean of the School of Architecture at MIT; Charles Killam, FAIA, professor at the Harvard School of Architecture; Mrs. James Jackson Storrow, president of Better Homes of America; Mrs. Thomas J. Walker, Massachusetts Federation of Women's Clubs; Miss Alice Blood, director of the School of Home Economics at Simmons College; Rodney Long, president of the Massachusetts Real Estate Exchange; and John T. Burns, Massachusetts Real Estate Exchange. It was said by the store that "the judges had great difficulty in the process of elimination. It was a herculean task, most conscientiously performed, and we deeply appreciate the efforts of the judges and thank each one of them." This competition was an important part of President Franklin Delano Roosevelt's National Recovery Act, and Jordan Marsh's role in sponsoring this competition provided not only the building (and furnishing) of seven houses but hopefully also a turning point in the economic recovery after the Great Depression and the suburban development taking place.

Richard Mitton, like his brother George W. Mitton before him, fully realized that as "Fellow Workers," the employees of Jordan Marsh were vitally important in the overall operation of the store, from the offices, sales floor, window decorating department, stock rooms, alteration rooms, receiving rooms, shipping rooms and innumerable departments with hundreds of people to the warehouses and shipping and receiving facilities. It was as if the store had a veritable army of employees who worked long days six days a week and were expected to extol the store motto, "The customer is always right," regardless of the circumstances involved. The Mittons, like the Jordans before them, realized that contented and well-remunerated employees were a vital part of the overall success of the store. With the establishment of a "library, smoking, reading and 'silence' rooms, a huge cafeteria, grill room and all the rest of it," Jordan Marsh was considered a wonderful and progressive place to work. In fact, there was a Training and Employment Department to ensure that new employees would work out, as well as an extensive Health Department and hospital for the well-being of the employees. There was also the Personnel Service Office, which would often allow Fellow Workers to rest at a house in Wrentham, Massachusetts. This was later increased to one house for women and another for men, which ironically was the house of Helen Adams Keller (1880–1968), the blind author and humanitarian. It was set on fifty acres and provided not just much-needed rest but also nutritious meals and care. Obviously, Jordan Marsh felt that a happy and contented employee was good for business.

In 1937, Edward Richardson Mitton succeeded his uncle as president of Jordan Marsh Company. A graduate of both Milton Academy and Harvard University, class of 1917, he was in essence trained to be president from the time of his youth. He joined Jordan Marsh Company in 1917, "starting work as a sales clerk behind a counter," but left to serve in the navy during World War I. Upon his return, he "rose to executive capacity through the roles of auxiliary merchandiser, divisional merchandise manager and general merchandise manager, becoming a director of the corporation…in 1924 and merchandising vice president [in]…1931." Dedicated to the store, it was said of him that he "preserved the good traditions of his forebears— pride in the organization, warmed by a determination to keep the best of old qualities alive."

Jordan Marsh, which had been founded in 1851 by Eben Jordan and Benjamin Marsh, was to celebrate its centennial in 1951. Mitton had a "clear vision and forceful determination which brought about the new construction era which inaugurates this turn of the Jordan Marsh century. In other words, his policy has been the best of the old must be continued and embodied in the new." Edward Mitton and his then board of directors, which included Cameron S. Thompson, Robert Mitton, Richard H. Edwards Jr., William A. Everett and James H. Fairclough Jr., commissioned the noted architectural firm of Perry, Shaw, Kehoe and Dean, which was based in Boston, to build their new store. Founded in 1923, the firm became notable for its designs for educational institutions. The firm was originally founded as Perry, Shaw and Hepburn and was responsible for the restoration of Colonial Williamsburg, thanks to the generosity of the Rockefeller family. The firm asserted its expertise in creating the context of a university environment. Perry, Shaw and Hepburn, Architects, as the firm was then known, had completed designing an entire college campus—master plan and individual buildings— for the Franklin W. Olin College of Engineering in Needham.

This Richard Mitton Memorial Award was presented in 1975 to Thomas Dunlay for the painting *The Ginger Jar*, which is now in the collection of the New Britain Museum of Art, New Britain, Connecticut. Begun in 1930 by Richard Mitton when he served as president of Jordan Marsh, the annual award was usually presented to the top seven artists receiving the most votes for their submitted paintings, along with a medal and cash prize. *Courtesy of Thomas Dunlay.*

In 1957, Robert Douglas Hunter received the Richard Mitton Memorial Award and a $250 check from Edward R. Mitton, who holds the Mitton Memorial Award, for his painting *Jerry*, which received the most votes in the twenty-seventh annual Jordan Marsh Exhibition of Paintings by Contemporary Artists in 1957.

By the 1940s, Perry, Shaw, Kehoe and Dean, Architects, as the firm was known from 1947 to 1952, was a fixture in the Boston architecture scene and had been commissioned for a series of important buildings in and around the city. Its initial concept for Jordan Marsh was to replace the older buildings between Summer, Chauncy and Avon Streets and create a massive department store that had the *touch and color and some details reminiscent of the period of 1800. In other words, brick by brick, this new store of Jordan's would take shape as a warm reminder of New England's [architectural] heritage and as a herald of the century to come. It would contain in its outward lines and shading the colonial spirit reflected in the red bricks of Faneuil Hall and of the old State House and all of the other structures where the talented Charles Bulfinch had left his mark. It would offer through its inner conveniences the peak efficiency of the 20th century.*

In 1947, Edward R. Mitton officially announced to the public that Jordan Marsh would build the greatest department store in the world. A statement was made in the local newspapers that caused tremendous excitement, and he was quoted as saying:

A decision has been reached which will exert its influence not only upon the future of this business, upon the local community of Boston, and upon the Commonwealth of Massachusetts, but also in fact to a degree upon the whole of New England. And so it is that with unbounded confidence in the integrity, stability and future prosperity of this area and community of peoples I am happy to announce our decision to commence a building program. This will be but another expression of our absolute confidence in the forward-looking spirit of the Boston and New England today.

In the years just after World War II, this was a major announcement and a sense of reinvestment in the city by Jordan Marsh that elicited widespread interest and confidence in the revitalization of downtown Boston. With a new store envisioned as covering a full city block, the area of Summer, Chauncy and Avon Streets, it was planned to have two sub-basements and fourteen stories. According to *Tales of the Observer*, there would be "talking elevators," with wire recorders announcing each floor and its contents. There would be fleximodule lighting, bringing a daylight glow to the broad aisles and the neat showcases. There would be air conditioning and automatic doorways, off-street ramps for trucks and trailers, miles of steel and aluminum to replace old-fashioned plaster and dust, block-long show windows, protective overhanging marquees, radiant-heated sidewalks that would cleanse themselves of snow and ice and a hundred other improvements and innovations. Perry, Shaw, Kehoe and Dean, in conjunction with Edward R. Mitton and the board of directors, would plan this new store to be built of red brick with white trim "in keeping with the

Margaret Leonie Mitton presents the Mitton Memorial Award to Robert Douglas Hunter for his painting *Reflections*, which won the competition in 1958. Mitton was the widow of Richard Mitton, the man for whom the award was named and who had served as president of Jordan Marsh from 1930 to 1937. They are seen at Locke-Ober Restaurant, where the luncheon in honor of Hunter was held.

rich dignity of early New England structures…[with the] touch and color of some details reminiscent of the period of 1800." With such a massive project, Jordan Marsh fully intended to remain in business while the work was done in steps, ensuring that once finished, the whole would be complete.

On May 21, 1949, the cornerstone was laid for the new building with great fanfare. It was a momentous occasion, as this new building was to commemorate the centennial of the founding of Jordan Marsh in 1851. United States senator Leverett Saltonstall presided at the ceremony, and Congressman John W. McCormack brought the congratulations of United States president Harry S. Truman. Edward R. Mitton, as the fifth president of Jordan Marsh since 1851, said at the ceremony:

> *This sturdy steel is synonymous of that strength of character for which both New England and Jordan's are famous. The red brick is representative of the warmth and friendliness of our New England people and of Jordan's.*

Above: "La Fiera Italiana" was held in 1960 at Jordan Marsh with Italian-themed merchandise and a fashion show held at the Sheraton Plaza to benefit Boys' Towns of Italy. Seen discussing the plans for the event are, *seated from left to right*, Monsignor John Patrick-Carroll, president of Boys' Towns of Italy; Mrs. Vincent Vallono, executive state chairman of Massachusetts Boys' Towns; Cameron S. Thompson, vice president of Jordan Marsh; Mrs. George Skouras, international chairman of Boys' Towns of Italy; *standing*: James H. Fairclough, vice president of Jordan Marsh; and Mrs. L. Von Arx, director of the national office of Boys' Towns of Italy.

Opposite, top: Jordan Marsh induced Captain Alan Villiers, captain of the *Mayflower*, to discuss his new book *Wild Ocean*, on the sailing of the second *Mayflower* across the Atlantic Ocean in 1957, at a luncheon and book signing at the store. Seen, *left to right*, are James Braim, buyer in the book department; Cameron S. Thompson, vice president of Jordan Marsh; and Captain Villiers.

Opposite, bottom: In 1960, Jordan Marsh sponsored "La Fiera Italiana," which was a two-week celebration to raise funds for the Boys' Towns of Italy with a fashion show at the Sheraton Plaza Hotel. Edward R. Mitton, president of Jordan Marsh, is on the far left, and he presented silver Paul Revere bowls to Mrs. George Skouras, international chairman of Boys' Towns of Italy; Alberto Fabiani, Italian couturier; Marchesa Antonello di Bugnano, carosa of Italy; Gaetano Savini Bironi, couturier; and Mrs. Vincent Vollono, chairman of Massachusetts Committee of Boys' Towns of Italy.

The New England granite is of the ruggedness and basic integrity of both our people and our institution. Its touches of modernism suggest the forward-looking principles which have always been the basis of New England process.

The cornerstone was to include a box in which was placed a history of Jordan Marsh, photographs of all the store's principals from Eben Dyer Jordan, current newspapers and currency, signatures of the members of the Half Century Club and the Quarter Century Club, the letter from President Truman and a print of the proposed new building. The justifiable pride of Mitton, his Fellow Workers, Bostonians and New Englanders was highly evident as it was declared that Jordan Marsh "will build the one store of its kind in all the world....It is the courage, the confidence, the serene and unshaken belief this old Boston institution has in Boston. It is the spirit of New England enterprise, a spirit undimmed as decade follows decade."

With such a massive building project, the steel beam to support the entire section of the new unit was produced at Bethlehem Steel in Pennsylvania and shipped to Boston on three contiguous railroad flatbeds. This was considered to be the largest steel beam ever produced up to that time at seventy-two feet in length and weighing seventy tons. The beam was placed on two low-bed trailers that were linked together and brought from the Southampton Street Railroad Yards to the building site with great fanfare. Bostonians watched with unabated interest in the project, from the two-story hole dug for the basements to the walls as they rose. It truly was the civic pride of Bostonians that was "born of the thought that the city's biggest department store was moving forward once again, this time into even broader fields than the past had known." Sensing that the public was a part of this, Jordan Marsh produced a button that had an image of "The Observer" that was given to all the supporters of the project who were to watch the construction through the specially cut peepholes in the wood fence along Chauncy Street or those who observed the progress from their office windows. When the addition was completed, it was not as originally planned, being somewhat reduced in size and scale, but still a marvelous addition to downtown Boston.

Boston Redevelopment Authority estimated that Jordan Marsh's total retail space at this time was 1,700,000 square feet, which made it overwhelmingly the largest retail venue in Boston. While the company was investing in its downtown store, it also began moving, along with its customers, to the suburbs. The process of shifting retail away from downtowns accelerated in the 1950s, with the first suburban store being at Shoppers World in Framingham. By 1957, the country had 940 shopping centers, most with at least one department store "anchor." Three years later, the number had doubled, and it doubled again in the next three years. By 1966, branch stores accounted for over half of all department store sales. Ten years later, more than three-quarters of total department store business nationwide came from branch sales.

The main building of Boston's Jordan Marsh complex, an ornate brownstone edifice with a landmark corner clock tower designed by Nathaniel J. Bradlee in the 1860s, was torn down in 1975, along with its entire row of historic Annex buildings. Local architect Leslie Larson founded a coalition called the City Conservation League to try to save the main building, which made way for a low-rise modern brick structure that sits there today as Macy's. It was said that some outraged customers cut up their credit cards in protest of the demolition. These protests and preservationist grass-roots efforts led to the creation of the Boston Landmarks Commission.

Over the next few years, it seemed as if Jordan Marsh began to languish as a department store. After Edward R. Mitton stepped down as president in 1962, there was a succession of presidents who served for only a few years each and did not create the sense of continuity that had been experienced under the Jordans and Mittons. With the shift from the flagship store to the suburban shopping malls, many people in Boston had begun to view Jordan Marsh as antiquated, old-fashioned and decidedly Victorian. Even the new addition designed by Perry, Shaw, Kehoe and Dean, Architects, seemed dated and outmoded, and the old sense of pride of place had begun to wane.

On December 19, 1994, Federated Department Stores acquired R.H. Macy & Co. and thereby created the world's largest department store company. Federated Department Stores operated more than 400 department stores and over 150 specialty stores in thirty-seven states. A&S Department Stores was acquired by Macy's in May 1995. Also in 1995, Federated Department Stores acquired the Broadway Department Stores, bringing Broadway, Emporium and Weinstocks to the Macy's chain of stores, as well as six former I. Magnin stores. It was said that about four dozen stores were converted to the Macy's name. Following the model of A&S, Jordan Marsh Department Stores of Boston, already owned by Federated Department Store, was sadly converted to Macy's in March 1996.

CHAPTER 6

THE ANNUAL THANKSGIVING DAY PARADE

Heralding the arrival of Santason, son of Santa Claus.

Beginning in 1929, the Jordan Marsh Company sponsored the Santason Parade in Boston. The idea of a Thanksgiving Day parade had been started by Macy's Herald Square, which was the largest store in the world following completion of the Seventh Avenue addition, in New York City. Since 1924, the Thanksgiving Day Parade, which was originally called the Macy's Christmas Parade, was a veritable flotilla of giant hot air balloons and bands accompanied by employees dressed as clowns and others in fanciful costumes and featuring live animals from the Central Park Zoo, all of which culminated with the appearance of Santa Claus at the end of the parade and the official beginning of the holiday shopping season.

However, in 1863 Abraham Lincoln, then president of the United States, proclaimed Thanksgiving Day, the fourth Thursday in November, to be observed as a national holiday. Ever since the Pilgrims had settled Plymouth Bay Colony in 1620, there had been seasonal communal feasts that showcased the vegetables and fruits of the season, with wild game and turkeys. By the mid-nineteenth century, Sarah Josepha Hale, a noted author and editor whose poem "Mary Had a Little Lamb" was widely known by children and adults nationwide, suggested that Thanksgiving should become a recognized national holiday. As the United States continued to grow in the late nineteenth century, with massive immigration to the country

The Thanksgiving Day Parade in 1931 was a massive one sponsored by Jordan Marsh and held in Boston. It was advertised as "heralding the impending arrival of the Yuletide Season." This strange insect-like balloon was paraded along Beacon Street with rope handlers dressed in fanciful costumes as Chinese, Arabians and Celtics, replete with spear and circular shields, as well as clowns.

that brought people of all walks of life, ethnicities, races and religion, the celebration of Thanksgiving was one that all Americans—new and old—could share in, with the addition of foods and desserts that were introduced to the country by new arrivals.

Like at Macy's Department Store in New York, George W. Mitton, president of Jordan Marsh Company in Boston, also thought that a parade on Thanksgiving Day morning would raise the morale of people who had recently begun to experience the effects of the Great Depression, which had begun only a month previously. The parade, which was touted by Acme News pictures as "heralding the impending arrival of the Yuletide Season… is staged in Boston, Mass., on Thanksgiving Day." On Thanksgiving Day 1929, a short parade was held from Copley Square along Beacon Street, down Park Street and Winter Street and arriving at Jordan Marsh. As huge rubber balloons that were filled with helium to keep them aloft, such

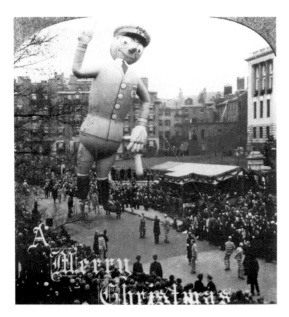

The Policeman SOS 13 balloon had been flown in Macy's New York Thanksgiving Day Parade in 1937 but the following year was sent to Jordan Marsh for its Santason Parade. It is seen here passing the reviewing stand in front of the Massachusetts State House, with the West Wing on the right, with handlers appropriately dressed in striped prison uniforms like escaped prison inmates in relation to the policeman balloon.

A cadre of smartly uniformed rope handlers guides a circular balloon with a seemingly disembodied head up Beacon Street. It seemed that the parade participants had as much fun as the thousands of Bostonians who lined the streets during the parade.

characters as the Blue Elephant and the Straw Man were led along the city streets lined with thousands of cheering Bostonians as they watched marching employees of Jordan Marsh, dressed in vibrant and fanciful costumes that ranged from clowns to Celtic warriors complete with shields and spears, Chinese men in traditional clothing and conical straw hats and Arabians in jackets with waist sashes and turbans, all of whom held tight the ropes that secured the floating balloons as they processed up Beacon Hill and then on to the department store.

As the marchers reached the department store at Washington and Summer Streets, the giant balloons were met with great fanfare and the rousing cheers of the thousands of Bostonians who had followed them along the streets. However, as planned, the Blue Elephant balloon was allowed to escape the grip of its holders and float into the horizon. The balloon had the return address of Jordan Marsh Company on the label that was sewn onto it, with prizes being offered for its safe return, as it was an expensive commodity to produce. The first year had unsuitable weather conditions on Thanksgiving Day, and only that one balloon, the Blue Elephant, was released. It was reported in a newspaper article to have "broke[n] away and headed out to sea. No word has been heard from it so that there are two rewards of $100 each to be claimed." A few weeks later, in the December 16 edition of the *Boston Daily Globe*, it was noted that the "Straw Man [balloon] is to be cut from his moorings! If YOU return him intact—you'll win the $100 reward—so—watch for him Saturday! He may fly YOUR way!" Well, with such massive publicity throughout Boston and the New England states, many people participated in the event that was judged by Jake Coolidge, editor of *Paramount News*, and George Hill of the *New York Times* and the Wide-World News Service. The winners, who were to receive prizes for movie clips or still photography of the balloons, were Wilbur Andrews of Newtonville for a movie prize and, for still photography, Fred Crosby of Somerville for third prize, E.H. Washburn of Dorchester for second prize and first-prize winner Arnold Mongiove of Dorchester. Each of the winners was presented a check by H.R. Clement of Jordan Marsh on the roof of the Jordan Marsh Annex as the Straw Man balloon oversaw the ceremony.

Throughout the 1930s, the Thanksgiving Day Santason Parade was widely marketed and continually expanded with new character balloons, some of which were sent by Macy's in New York from its previous year's balloons. The parade would eventually begin at Kenmore Square and process along Beacon Street, a three-mile walk, turning east on Park Street in front of the Massachusetts State House, where a tented reviewing stand

Above: The Big Indian balloon had been flown in the Macy's New York Thanksgiving Day Parade in 1935 and "was billed by the advance agent as super colossal, and he was.... His fierce painted eyes stared...and [he] was given, at moments, to a peculiar tribal dance to which his body swayed from side to side." A police band precedes the balloon, with thousands of parade attendees lining both sides of the parade route.

Opposite, top: A kangaroo balloon passes up Beacon Street as people not only watch from windows and balconies of the Beacon Hill townhouses but also throng the sidewalks.

Opposite, bottom: A two-headed giant balloon—with two heads that seem to look in each direction, replete with pierced ears, head bandannas and holding a spiked mace—had flown in Macy's New York Thanksgiving Day Parade in 1936 and was seen here on Summer Street in Boston the following year. The twenty-person-deep crowds overflow the sidewalks and could not have been more excited as the balloon passed Jordan Marsh on Summer Street with Filene's and Kennedy's Department Stores seen on the right.

was always erected, and along Winter Street until it reached Jordan Marsh; other years, the parade route was from South Station along Kneeland Street and Tremont Street down Court to Washington Street. With the increased parade route came new balloons that were said to be, in some cases, "strange figures," such as centipedes, insects, kangaroos, pigs, a double-headed giant with a spiked mace and a policeman. With each new balloon, one needed a minimum of twelve strapping men to hold the guide ropes, and to add to the already stretched number of available employees of the department store, there were many people who were hired for a few dollars just for the day and were dressed in fanciful costumes. In fact, in 1934, the *Harvard Crimson* placed an advertisement that stated, "Harvard students, dressed as Santa Clauses, will march in the annual 'Santason' parade, sponsored by Jordan Marsh Department store on Thanksgiving morning. Each student who marches in the parade which will start from the South Station and march through Boston will be paid $3.00. Any students who wish to apply should do so at the Student Employment office in University Hall." The Santason Parade was to prove one of the most popular holiday events of the year and was avidly anticipated by children and adults alike.

In the late 1930s, the *Boston Globe* created a fervor of excitement by stating that "Santason, mythical son of Santa Claus is coming to town!" He was due to depart Santa's North Pole workshop and reach Esquimeauxland (obviously the land where Eskimos lived), where he would then board a tri-motored plane that would arrive in Boston at the Charles River Basin near the Union Boat Club. The year 1938 was the first one that Santason, according to the newspaper, had "flown from a point so near the North Pole." Santason would be spectacularly dressed in a red cloth two-piece suit with a white fur-edged hat, sleeve cuffs, coat edging and boot tops, as well as a wide leather belt with a crossed leather harness across his chest. "In the past he has mushed to Nome, Alaska, and taken to the air," as there was said to be no suitable landing field nearer to the Pole than Nome, so at "the suggestion of Santa Claus, a field was laid out during the warm season and a hangar built for the plane. Several rotary plows and skis were brought to the field to insure Santason's departure should there be snow on the ground," with a crew of three, including a co-pilot, navigator and radio operator. "Santason himself will be the chief pilot....In addition to being a pilot, Santason is a licensed radio operator and will relieve the radio man." To cover the plane's progress, the General Television Company in Boston and local radio broadcasting studios would follow his travels over the "20-meter wave length and television" and report to an excited and anxious audience.

All of this hoopla, hype and excitement led up to Thanksgiving Day, when Santason duly arrived and the Thanksgiving Day parade officially began.

When World War II began in the United States with the bombing of Pearl Harbor, all Americans quickly drew together to jointly support the war effort, as well as the men and women serving in the armed forces both in Europe and in the Pacific Campaign. Jordan Marsh was to regretfully suspend the Thanksgiving Day Santason Parade in 1943, stating in the *Boston Daily Globe* on November 25, 1943, "We too, are sorry there will be no Santason Parade this year." The long-heralded parade was suspended due to a shortage of gasoline, rubber and the helium that made the balloons float high, all of which were desperately needed for the war effort. Bostonians were undoubtedly disappointed, and the newspaper cancellation notice stated, "We loved it as much as you did. The fun and noise, the merriment. The great balloons and clowns and floats and all the bands. You and one million like you, packing Boston's streets and trains and subways and taxis… all coming to welcome Santa and Santason when he came to Jordan's." Though there was no parade, it was said that "Santa and Santason have come to Jordan's without the bands.…They're in New England's largest Toyland right now," which happened to be the seventh-floor toy department at Jordan Marsh. Though the parade had become a beloved tradition, it was an important and patriotic decision to suspend it, and Jordan Marsh asked the public to "buy War Stamps and Bonds and work hard for Victory—and the biggest Parade then, EVER."

CHAPTER 7

THE ENCHANTED VILLAGE
OF SAINT NICHOLAS

Everyone *remembers the Enchanted Village—my children too.*
—Jeannette Genova

As *Look* magazine said in December 1959, "Once there was an old-fashioned Christmas, but it got lost. Green trees turned pink and were trimmed with mink. This year, a return to traditionalism, typified by Bavarian-looking children's clothes, new 'old-fashioned' tree ornaments and German goodies, will help revive the season's warmth. *Look* observed this trend recently at Jordan Marsh, a leading Boston store, where an 'enchanted village' recaptures the mood of *Gemutlichkeit*."

The Enchanted Village at the Jordan Marsh Department Store was the realization of an old-fashioned Victorian-themed display that delighted not just the children of Boston but also their parents and grandparents, who viewed with a mesmerized awe the wonderful displays with their automated figures. Following World War II, Jordan Marsh Company decided not to resume the Santason Parade on Thanksgiving Day to announce the beginning of the holiday season. Though it had been tremendously popular and an immensely successful marketing strategy, the war had put an end to the parade in 1943, and the store decided to use the plate-glass display windows facing Summer and Washington Streets not only for store merchandise but also for window displays of holiday cheer. A new multistory addition to Jordan Marsh had been designed by the noted Boston architectural firm of Perry, Shaw, Kehoe and Dean and was built to suitably commemorate the

The Hofmann-built glassblower in the Ornament Shop in the Enchanted Village of Saint Nicholas was photographed by *Look* magazine in December 1959 with three children admiring the multicolored ornaments, which are of blown glass and decorated with traditional Bavarian designs.

centennial of Jordan Marsh in 1951. With wide plate-glass windows allowing ample display space for passing shoppers to stop and view, it also had a wide parapet that extended over Summer and Chauncy Streets that provided cover during inclement weather and was also to become the area where a life-sized nativity scene was annually displayed. With illuminations in the evening, especially on nights when the store was open late for shoppers, and bells tolling along with Christmas music, it was seen from all directions with its huge backboard of palm trees with illuminated stars and the brilliant Star of Bethlehem that surmounted the montage.

However, Edward Mitton, president of Jordan Marsh, wanted something that was more on the scale of the former Santason Thanksgiving Day Parade. Conferring with his store managers and staff, he learned of the Christian Hofmann Company in Bad Rodach, a town in Coburg in Upper Franconia, West Germany, that created lifelike reproductions of animated display figures for a wide variety of venues—among them leisure parks, museums and department stores. The concept of the Enchanted Village of Saint Nicholas was something that would involve an entire Victorian village of shops such as a toymaker shop, a wigmaker shop, a glassblower shop, a schoolhouse, a bakery and a blacksmith shop, all of which created a sense of nostalgia for the Christmases of days gone by and was also an attraction for the thousands of New Englanders who nostalgically remembered the Thanksgiving Day parades. As William Bird suggested in his book *Holidays on Display*, the miniature architecture of the Christmas villages tended to be a mixture of Tudor Revival and storybook style, with half-timbering and mullioned windows that mimicked medieval cottages and English country houses. The twee buildings and people in the villages made you feel as if you were walking through a storybook because literature was the most common vehicle for entertainment.

Christian Hofmann had begun as a toy factory in 1878 in Bad Rodach, Coburg, Germany, and became so popular that it would provide toys to the Duke of Coburg. By the mid-twentieth century, the company expanded when Hans-Joachim Hofmann, the grandson of the founder, joined the family company. The company saw larger sheds built in the early 1950s, and with this increased space, it began to produce animated figures that caught the attention of those in both Europe as well as the United States. These animated figures were then considered state-of-the-art, and according to the company history, the "figures and animals are produced according to the wishes of our customers, in double robust mechanics and with the suitable kind of drive. Then the most modern digital electronics breathes life into the 'little robots.'" Edward Mitton felt sure that the public would react positively to the concept of this village, and it was ordered for the Boston flagship store of Jordan Marsh. The Enchanted Village was not just to be animated figures and animals but an entire village that was built to a child's scale, which allowed views into the houses and shops where figures would be seen moving to and fro.

The work on the village began in March 1959. Christian Hofmann must have realized that this commission, by the largest department store in New England, was certainly the largest in its eighty-year history. Granted, it was among the best toy makers in Germany, but this order from Jordan Marsh was to have over 250 automated figures of adults and children with over sixteen thousand mechanical parts and four thousand feet of wire, innumerable motors for moving parts as well as gallons of paint, which allowed the painters to create the two dozen scenes. The company had to hire additional help, not just carpenters but also electrical engineers, doll makers, people to sew the costumes and painters who were to create the charming and nostalgia-filled scenes of a Christmas past. The painstaking work and

Right: Two young girls peer into the bake shop with a Hofmann-built baker in the Enchanted Village of Saint Nicholas that was photographed by *Look* magazine in December 1959. Trays of Bavarian-inspired cookies, a gingerbread house and other German Christmas treats including nusshaufchen, spekulatius, pfeffernusse and spitzkuchen were displayed in the bakery window—and also sold during the holiday season in the Jordan Marsh Bakery.

Below: The Hofmann-built schoolmaster in the schoolhouse of the Enchanted Village of Saint Nicholas is surrounded by children in the *Look* magazine photograph of December 1959. In essence, the children created an impromptu Christmas party in the school, as the automated schoolmaster oversees the festivities.

attention to detail was certainly nothing new to Christian Hofmann, but with the work being done on such a large scale it was nothing less than remarkable. Though the Enchanted Village of Saint Nicholas at Jordan Marsh was the first display of its kind completed by Christian Hofmann, it was quickly followed in 1961 with the Enchanted Colonial Village that was produced for Lit Brothers in Philadelphia and, later, the Dickens Village for Strawbridge and Clothier in Philadelphia. Even Gimbel's Department Store got in on the act. Once the village and its many-figured assemblage was finished, it was crated and shipped from the port of Bremerhaven, Germany, to Boston and was brought to the Jordan Marsh Annex, a multistory building adjacent to the Main Store, on the opposite side of Avon Street. There, the Enchanted Village of Saint Nicholas was uncrated and set up according to the precise instructions of the Christian Hofmann Company.

A craftsman at the Christian Hofmann Company in Coburg, West Germany, is seen in 1959 painting the face and body of one of the automated figures being produced for the Enchanted Village of Saint Nicholas. Jordan Marsh had commissioned hundreds of figures, from adults and children to every animal imaginable. Notice the upside-down heads strung on a line drying after having been painted before they are assembled.

The Enchanted Village of Saint Nicholas was a "mixture of Tudor Revival and storybook style, with half-timbering and mullioned windows that mimicked medieval cottages and English country houses." Seen from the walkway, the façades had automated figures that peeked from doors and windows, as well as a cat that sat on the chimney top. Notice the village jail on the right.

The area allotted for the creation of the Enchanted Village was an eight-thousand-square-foot space in the Annex, accessible by the public by both elevator and escalator. The village that had been created in West Germany was truly a village in every sense of the word, with a schoolhouse, bakery, cobbler shop, tailor shop, watchmaker shop and village store, all of which was to come to life when the switch was turned on and the four-foot, eight-inch figures—in addition to horses, dogs, cats and ducklings—all began to move in unison. One scene showed a woman reading a book in a library, another a dog eating a string of popcorn from a Christmas tree, another Mrs. Claus rolling out dough in a kitchen and another a boy seated in a barbershop getting a haircut. When Jordan Marsh began to publicize the upcoming opening of the Enchanted Village in the fall of 1959, the anticipation and excitement that was created was tremendous. From the local newspapers to a letter sent to Jordan Marsh customers, Edward Mitton said, "We have created this year the Enchanted Village of Saint Nicholas. First of its kind in the world...with its wonderful animated characters that will delight all children and adults." Beginning in early November, the workers began to uncrate the wonderful animated characters, and the three-hundred-foot-long village began to come to life.

The day following Thanksgiving was the gala opening day, and huge lines of children accompanied by adults waited in long queues to enter this newly created winter wonderland, replete with festive poinsettias, holly kissing balls and over two dozen scenes that one could watch, in amazement, as every one of the scenes had some form of animation, including a poignant one of a young Louisa Barreis purchasing a yard of cherry-red ribbon from a bewhiskered figure of Eben Dyer Jordan himself in 1841, the first sale in his Hanover Street store. Visitors would walk through the village, with stanchions on either side, with twelve-foot-high snow-covered buildings and "see holiday decorating taking place through the windows of homes, toy-making going on through a storefront window, and figures in other buildings getting ready for the holidays and enjoying the season." So successful had the marketing of this village been through newspapers, radio and television that on its dedication, Edward Mitton would say of the Enchanted Village of Saint Nicholas that "this delightful, authentic panorama, with its wonderful animated characters at work and play, is for the enjoyment of all children and adults. We hope it will cast a spell of enchantment over all our New England friends...adding to a brighter, gayer, more delightful Christmas season." And so it did, tenfold.

The music room at the Enchanted Village of Saint Nicholas had a traditionally dressed Hofmann-built Santa Claus playing traditional Christmas carols on the piano as children appeared in windows above with musical instruments, all of which added to the festive music being played for the holidays. In the 1960s, a trio of musicians—John Christoforo, Danny Cavicchio and Charles Opper—dressed in lederhosen and Tyrolean hats played music, along with an organist who played traditional hymns to entertain the throngs of visitors.

For Bostonians throughout the 1960s and 1970s, visiting the Enchanted Village during the holiday season was a rite of passage, and it attracted people of all ages, all walks of life and, remarkably, all religions. The anticipation of seeing the village was something that brought masses of people to Jordan Marsh. In the weeks leading up to Christmas, the department store hired new seasonal employees who dressed as Santa's helpers and elves who not only staffed the ticket booth at the corner of Summer and Chauncy Streets, adjacent to the Fellow Workers' entrance, but also helped to direct the thousands of visitors who came on a daily basis (many thousands on the weekends) and forged cherished memories of this revered Christmas tradition. As Donna Korman said, "We stood in long, long lines when this opened. It was so festive, Christmas music and all the scenes—I loved it!" After walking through the village, "visitors would find Santa Claus and elves.…Children would be given a candy cane and have the chance to speak with Santa. And in recent times, festive holiday

Children peer through the wood stanchions along the walkway to see the exhibits, and their parents are equally charmed by the attention to detail, watching the automated elves in the foreground. As it really was intended to be a village, even automated cows, horses, dogs and sheep were part of the Enchanted Village of Saint Nicholas. Here, under a small wood-shingled shed, the animals would move in unison, creating a bucolic barn scene as people passed through the village.

music was played, the music of the Boston Pops Orchestra." Even the locally popular television star Rex Trailer was at the village; his visit was to be included in *Rex Trailer Boomtown Gold*.

Popular and extremely well attended for many years, the magic of the Enchanted Village of Saint Nicholas unfortunately began to wane in the early 1970s, and Jordan Marsh discontinued the annual holiday display in 1972. According to Daniel White, "Jordan Marsh put the village in storage in 1972 and after a few years sold it. All or part of it found its way to, I think, the Liberty Tree Mall in Danvers. It was pretty beaten up at this point, so only a few of the props and animated display figures were put out on display in the hallways of the mall." After Macy's purchased Jordan Marsh, it decided to reestablish the beloved Boston Christmas tradition, and it was reopened to the public. However, Jordan Marsh had "contracted with a store mannequin company in the U.S. This company had never made animated figures before, so they had to make it all up from scratch." It was to resume as a popular and well-attended attraction for the next few years, but Macy's soon realized that it was not proving to be as great a draw as it once had been. In 1998, Macy's donated what was left of the Enchanted Village to the City of Boston, as Mayor Thomas M. Menino had expressed an interest in helping to preserve the now three-decade-old tradition by creating a seasonal display on Boston City Hall Plaza in a temporary building. After only five years, the tremendous expense of maintaining the village had become an increased burden on the city, and with not only staffing problems but also a lower-than-anticipated attendance, as well as a lack of funding support from city institutions, the city transferred the village to the John B. Hynes Veterans Memorial Convention Center on Boylston Street in Boston's Back Bay. Here, the Enchanted Village of Saint Nicholas would remain until 2006, when it was placed in storage.

In January 1960, a citation was presented to Edward R. Mitton of Jordan Marsh from the chamber of commerce of Coburg, West Germany, for the furthering of closer ties between the United States and West Germany. *From left to right:* Guenthar Motz, West German consul for New England; Edward R. Mitton, president of Jordan Marsh; Hans Joachim Hofmann, head of Christian Hofmann Company; and Edward Schmidt, chamber of commerce of Coburg, West Germany. The Enchanted Village of Saint Nicholas was a huge success and brought great publicity to the store.

In May 2009, the surviving figures and accoutrements of the Enchanted Village were put up for auction by Stanley J. Paine Auctioneers, and the lot was purchased by Jordan's Furniture and was restored to its former glory and put on display during the holiday season at the Avon, Massachusetts store. Eliot Tatelman, then chief executive officer of Jordan's Furniture, said, "If you lived around here, everyone went to Jordan Marsh," not just because it was the largest department store in New England but also because it was a special place during the holidays. When Tatelman won the auction, which had bids starting at $25,000, he beat out six other bidders in an auction that lasted all of eight minutes. He spent a total of $161,000 because the sale included a 15 percent buyer's premium to pay for the cost of the auction and to fund the restoration and refurbishment of the figures, animals and village façades. Tatelman said, "I felt very compelled to do this because this is a New England thing; how could we not keep it going? I'm very excited to take responsibility of this tradition, and it will be featured in the holiday display at our Avon store."

The window displays along the Summer Street façade of Jordan Marsh had magical Christmas-themed displays with signs that read, "See the Enchanted Village of Saint Nicholas," as well as instructions to see and visit Toyland at Jordan Marsh's fifth floor in the Annex, which was New England's largest display of toys.

A miniature illuminated Victorian village was created in the huge display windows along the Washington Street façade of Jordan Marsh and brought thousands of people to see it day and night. After the Santason Parade ended in 1943, Jordan Marsh created these wonderful windows of holiday cheer that proved immensely popular.

The original location of the life-sized Nativity scene was on the parapet that curved around the corner of Chauncy and Summer Streets. Set in a rustic stone arched grotto, surmounted by the Star of Bethlehem, were Mary, Joseph and the baby Jesus, seen in the center, with the three wise men on the right and shepherds on the left, along with their flock of sheep along the sides. This huge scene could be seen from Summer Street and was within walking distance of the Arch Street Shrine, where many who worked as well as shopped in town would stop for Mass or for confessions.

By the mid-1960s, the Nativity scene had been moved to the parapet along the Summer Street façade. The earlier painted palm trees were replaced with three-dimensional ones, and twinkling electric stars and recorded holiday music were added to get shoppers in the holiday mood. The old Charlestown Savings Bank can be seen just past Chauncy Street, along with the Summer Street streetscape.

Tatelman also wanted to include the once famous Jordan Marsh blueberry muffins, and through John Pupek, a former baker at Jordan Marsh, the "whole experience, memories of the village and the muffins have made some visitors cry." The Enchanted Village, once a holiday mainstay at the Jordan Marsh flagship store in Boston in the 1960s, has become the pride of place at Jordan's Furniture in Avon, Massachusetts, during the holiday season. Thanks to Eliot Tatelman and the store, the Enchanted Village of Saint Nicholas continues to delight New Englanders in the twenty-first century, and as Edward Mitton so poignantly said at its dedication in 1959, "its wonderful animated characters…will delight all children and adults."

JORDAN MARSH TOYLAND

Toyland at Jordan Marsh was on the fifth floor of the Annex and was a place that was like the veritable holy grail for the children of New England. Jordan

114

Marsh had always stocked a wide array of toys since the nineteenth century, but by the mid-twentieth century, it seemed as if every toy available could be found at Toyland. At the time the Annex was built, Jordan Marsh advertised it as the "Headquarters for Santa Claus" and said, "Our Great Toy Section in our NEW BUILDING is by far the Largest and Best Stocked Toy Store in Boston."

There were educational toys for preschool children that included a Holgate Rocky Color Cone, a Playskool Nok-out Bench, a Playskool Postal Station, a Musical Sweeper and a Looky Chug-Chug train. These and many other toys were not only fun but also educational, as they helped in the formation of sensory aspects such as hearing, touch or taste.

Little boys might be mesmerized by the Lionel and American Flyer train sets that could actually puff smoke as well as whistle as they rounded the track. Not only were there a locomotive and hopper car but also an oil car, tender, gondola car and red caboose. With a wide selection of accessories, a train set could be added to with a hopper car and coal ramp, which could actually dump coal into a coal bin; a cattle car and corral that had nine head of cattle; and a milk car with a platform complete with metal milk pails. Extra accessories might include a water tower, highway flasher or additional track that made the train set even more impressive. There were race car sets, toy soldiers, miniature ships, model airplanes and car models. A boy might possibly want a Roy Rogers Cowboy outfit or a Hopalong Cassidy cowhide double holster and pistols with a cowboy hat or even, like Joe Cedrone, a Howdy Doody doll that was a "red-haired, freckle-faced rascal dressed in bright Western-style togs!" There were also Radio Steel wagons, Bull Dog Dump Trucks and red firetrucks with a real bell among other things.

Little girls might be enchanted with Madame Alexander dolls that were dressed in fine dresses and hats. Also available were the Baby Belle Doll, the Dydee Doll, the Sweetie Pie, the Toni Doll, Effanbee's "Mommy's Baby Doll" with a lifelike crying voice and the ultimate: the Madame Alexander's Bride Doll, which was dressed like a traditional bride in a "white nylon, wispy veil...even the blue garter and pink fingernail polish." It seemed as if there was such a wide assortment of dolls that no child would be displeased. The Marx Doll Houses came in both seven- and five-room models, and all the furniture was a miniature version of home. Cameo tea sets allowed children to serve tea to friends and dollies, and maybe after tea the doll could be taken for a stroll in the doll stroller with "leatherette fabric body, peek-a-boo hood, sun visor, and duchess gears."

There were "Little Miss Florence Nightingale" nurse's outfits, complete with a navy cape and nurse's cap, and a Dale Evans Cowgirl outfit. There were toy ironing boards, a toy cleaning set and a dolly bath for the child to emulate her mother.

For both children, Toyland offered Hansel and Gretel puppet theaters, marionettes, telescopes, Radio Steel red wagons, a Fleetwing Racer sled, a bicycle with training wheels and, for the youngest child, a Junior Velocipede. There were games such as Clue, Sorry, Captain Video Space and Hopalong Cassidy, as well as erector sets, chemistry sets and microscope sets. Of course, toys came in a wide range of prices, but Jordan Marsh conveniently offered a budget payment plan and suggested that one use their store charge account to save time.

Jordan Marsh would also host prominent authors with book signings in the Book Department in the Annex, as well as stars of the theater and television. Joe Cedrone attended a highly publicized event where Sophia Loren appeared before more than one thousand people at Jordan Marsh in 1979, and he was given a signed publicity photograph of the star after meeting her. She was at Jordan Marsh publicizing her new perfume, Sophia. Edward H. Land, the founder of Polaroid Corporation, appeared in 1948 at Jordan Marsh demonstrating his Polaroid Land Camera that took instant photographs. Hundreds of people came to see this revolutionary way to capture the moment. "Fifty-seven [cameras] were put up for sale at Boston's Jordan Marsh department store before the 1948 Christmas holiday....All fifty-seven cameras and all the film were sold on their first day of demonstrations." In 1938, the "world's Largest Collection of Smallest Curiosities" was held to display Jules Charbneau's collection of 25,800 miniatures, from the smallest scissors and smallest dictionary to the smallest painting in the world. These events were a vitally important way of attracting Bostonians to visit the store. Other events included lectures, art shows and demonstrations that hopefully would translate to sales. Even the Bunratty Castle Singers from Shannon, Ireland, appeared in 1988 to a huge audience and great review.

Jordan Marsh prepared letters in 1925 from Santa Claus that were sent to All the Children in the World from Santa's Toy Shop in the North Pole, in care of Jordan Marsh Company. What child would not be over-the-moon excited to receive a personal letter from Santa Claus, postmarked Sugar-Plum, North Pole?

This festive gift box was often under New Englanders' Christmas trees in the 1960s. Most people thought the four-in-hand Tally-Ho was extremely picturesque and festive, especially with the outrider and his trumpet. If shoppers wanted something extra special, there was a gift wrapping department, where one could choose simple or elaborate wrapping paper and bows to delight the gift recipient.

A huge three-dimensional Santa Claus opens the book *Tales from Mother Goose* at the tower on the corner of Washington Street and Avon Street as characters from the book's stories are seen to emerge. The colored neon sign just above the store entrance directs children and adults with a red arrow "To New England's Largest Toyland," which was on the fifth floor of the Annex.

A couple with their two young sons stop to admire airplane models and a ship model in Toyland at Jordan Marsh. The selection of toys available was incredible, and during the holiday season, Toyland was the place to be for children and their companions.

A sales clerk, *left*, seems somewhat dazed by the large number of shoppers in Toyland during the holiday season in 1965. The clerk wraps twine around a Battleground Play Set so the shopper can carry it home with ease.

A large model train set with curving tracks that encircle styrofoam hills and goes through tunnels and over trestle bridges attracted the undivided attention of children, teenagers and adults. These model train sets would be set up with complete villages and other realistic scenes to hopefully attract customers to purchase them, all the while entertaining a wide array of people in Toyland.

A very lucky boy or girl would be thrilled to receive an American Flyer train set, which had an engine and coal car, hopper car, boxcar, gondola car and red caboose. This train set included twelve feet of track and a twenty-five-watt transformer with an "easy-grip Speed Throttle and durable case" and was available at Jordan Marsh's Toyland, as were accessories to create a larger display.

A car racing set, complete with road-bed sections that allowed the sports cars to be raced, was a great attraction for shoppers, as it was an action-packed set that no child (and some adults) could refuse. The children on the left are mesmerized by the race cars that sped to the finish line. It was like a miniature Indy 500 in the comfort of one's own home.

The Christmas 1950 Jordan Marsh catalogue depicted Santa Claus chatting with children in their living room as they play with an Armored Bank Truck, a Hopalong Cassidy cowhide double pistol and holster and a lovely Madame Alexander doll. Jordan Marsh Company offered "Christmas Gifts for All the Family from New England's Largest Store." Gifts could be bought in the store or ordered and shipped to one's home.

121

Left: The noted artist Norman Rockwell depicted in a Christmas advertisement two pajama-clad children in a big wing chair on Christmas Eve who had fallen asleep waiting for Santa Claus. Santa Claus peeks from behind the wing chair, with his bag full of toys and candy canes, as elves caution him to be quiet so as not to awaken the children. *Courtesy of Carolyn Thornton.*

Right: The Jordan Marsh Great Basement Store had great toy values that were "fun-filled, play-packed gifts for every child on your list!" From a battery-operated Chi-Chi the Chihuahua or Mr. Fix-It Tool Belt to the Patti-Cake Doll, there was literally something for everyone.

CHAPTER 8

FELLOW WORKERS

The spirit of organization is what counts most.
—*Eben Dyer Jordan Jr.*

There is a bronze plaque near the Fellow Workers' entrance to the former Jordan Marsh Department Store on Chauncy Street in Boston that was dedicated on May 13, 1951, to George W. Mitton (1888–1947), president of Jordan Marsh Company from 1916 to 1930. It declares in Mitton's own words: "Hereinafter there shall be no such term as a Jordan Marsh employee, from here on, we are all fellow workers regardless of our position with the company."

It was a magnanimous and kind gesture by the president of the store, but it was also that fact that Jordan Marsh Company had often referred to as the "House of Progress." In *The Story of a Store*, it was said that "the policy of this store is to fill positions of trust and responsibility by advancing those in their employ wherever possible. Practically all the buyers and other executive heads have grown up in the store."

When one thinks of Jordan Marsh's Fellow Workers, the sales clerk obviously comes to mind, as they were so omnipresent in the stores, but the jobs available at the store were wide and varied and showed a real concern for the well-being and contentment of the employee. There was "an immense amount of detail connected with the purchasing, accounting, bookkeeping, checking and billing. The office help alone forms a small army." There were offices for auditing, retail, mail order and receiving,

George W. Mitton (1888–1947) started as a young clerk at Jordan Marsh and would rise to the presidency following the death of Eben Dyer Jordan Jr. in 1916. He coined the term "Fellow Workers" with regard to Jordan Marsh employees. This bronze plaque was dedicated on May 13, 1951, and was mounted near the Fellow Workers' entrance on Chauncy Street.

Marie Taff Mitton and Edward R. Mitton, *left*, present $1,000 checks at a banquet at the Imperial Ballroom of the Hotel Statler in Boston for new Jordan Marsh Half Century Club members. *Left to right*: Agatha L. McMullin, Anna E. Murphy and Katherine M. Roche. These three ladies were inducted into the prestigious club, founded in 1922, for those who were employed at Jordan Marsh for fifty years. Members of the Half Century Club also received platinum service pins with five diamonds.

but there was also "the great Alteration Room where women's and children's garments may be altered if necessary; Sponging Room; the Corset Alteration Room; the Cobbler Shop; Men's Busheling Room where the men's and boy's garments are altered; Men's Cravat Manufacturing Room; Embroidery Work Rooms where fancy embroidery is done; Fur Workroom featuring cleaning, repairing and custom order work of furs; Jewelry and Silverware Repairing and Engraving; Doll Repairing; Picture Framing; Brass Buffing; Paint Shop; Sign Painters Shop; Oriental Rug Repairing by native Armenians; Carpet Sewing; Upholstery, Window Shade, Drapery and Awning Manufacturing; Carpenter Shop; Machine Shop; and Electrical Shop. In the Atlas Storehouse Mattress and Box Spring making is done." Incredible as it seems, Jordan Marsh Company was not just the fabric of life for shoppers, it wove that fabric!

The Jordan Marsh Half Century Club met in 1943 in the Imperial Ballroom of the Hotel Statler in Boston. George W. Mitton, chairman of the Jordan Marsh board of directors, is seen standing on the far left. New members of the club are, *seated from left to right*, Katherine J. Sutton, Helen M. Egan and Elizabeth L. Daley; *standing from left to right*: Edward J. Pendergast, Anna F. Tobin, Joseph J. Howard and John W. Kenney.

Jordan Marsh showed a care and concern for its Fellow Workers who, in many cases, had longevity with the store that was incredible. In 1919, W.A. Hawkins, with the full support of George W. Mitton, founded the Quarter Century Club for employees who had worked at the store for twenty-five years. They would receive a solid gold pin with five blue stars. In 1922, the Half Century Club was founded for employees with fifty years of service; they received a bonus of $1,000 and a platinum pin with five diamonds. This was undoubtedly one of the major reasons for the success of Jordan Marsh, and an annual banquet was held for members and those to be newly inducted into each august group. To safeguard the well-being of their Fellow Workers, a Health Department was established in the Bristol Building that offered a doctor and five nurses, with three office employees, who at no charge saw ill employees from 9:30 a.m. to 5:30 p.m. daily. According to Judith Sumner, the daughter-in-law of a Jordan Marsh nurse:

> *The nurses also dealt in tea and sympathy, providing comfort for overly tired shoppers and lonely souls who may have felt faint or demoralized. The nurses also functioned as de facto store "mothers" doling out advice on finances and common sense to young employees....When I became engaged to her son in 1975, the nurses clearly wanted to "look me over" to make sure that I was suitable daughter-in-law material. I won them over by hand-delivering homemade Christmas cookies to the department.*

There was also a dentist who was present from Tuesday to Friday mornings, and a dental hygienist was in the office daily, with only a nominal fee being charged. A chiropodist was also in the office on Friday mornings, which must have been a boon for the employees who spent all day on their feet. Ill employees recovering at home saw a company visiting nurse.

Jordan Marsh established a credit union in 1931 that allowed employees to save and also to borrow at a low interest for major purchases such as a home or an automobile. The Mutual Aid Association was also something that provided support for employees who had extended medical care, with salary up to twenty-six weeks. And to preclude that employees were content and well fed, a Fellow Workers Cafeteria and the Grill Room were on the ninth floor of the Annex, where low-cost but highly nutritious foods were available, as well as a fully stocked library and a silence room where Fellow Workers could relax in a comfortable space.

As *The Story of a Store* justifiably boasted:

This is a vast business that has been built by deserving the confidence placed in it by the people. It has always given its customers value, dollar for dollar, and righted any reasonable wrong. Such shall always be the policy of this house and it shall be a constant endeavor to perfect the store, the system, the policy and the merchandise if the customer can be benefited thereby. It is an institution known as the representative Boston store throughout this country and Europe—founded and managed by New England people.

Among the Fellow Workers of Jordan Marsh "brought together under one name by those sound policies which were established 100 years ago in this little wholesale store on Milk Street" were the following.

THE CHRISTOFOROS

John Christoforo and his father, John Christoforo, were employed at Jordan Marsh in the mid-twentieth century, and both had fond memories of working at the department store.

The younger John Christoforo is the son of John and Angelina (known as Anne) Contini Christoforo, and he was raised on Eagle Hill in East Boston, attending local schools. He graduated from English High School. During his college years at Boston State, he worked at Jordan Marsh in inventory control and inter-department deliveries, or, as he said, "I was a hamper pusher." He continued his education with a master's degree from Boston State, as well as Harvard University, and later a doctorate from Boston University. An educator in Boston with a part-time job at the Seville Theater, as well as a popular and well-known musician in Boston for over fifty years, he played for the Uniques, a Motown group from the soul/Motown days, under his name Johnny Christy, where he "led everything from trios to eighteen-piece dance orchestras over the years." He also was to become a popular character actor for Hollywood's Paramount Studios.

His father, John, was also a talented musician and was the leader of a trio of musicians that played at the Enchanted Village of Saint Nicholas from 1959 when it opened through the mid-1960s. The trio was associated with Guy Ormandy, a well-known bandleader at the Sherry Biltmore Hotel on Massachusetts Avenue in Boston's Back Bay, and was composed of John Christoforo, who played the bass violin and the tuba; Charles Opper, who played the violin; and Danny Cavicchio, who played the accordion.

The trio was appropriately dressed in lederhosen and Tyrolean hats and "looked like farmers from Austria and Switzerland," according to John's son, which created a sense of *Gemutlichkeit* to complement the German-themed Enchanted Village. Their music provided a wonderful backdrop to the thousands who visited the popular venue.

The Christoforoses' music has long been appreciated in Boston, and it was a vital part of Jordan Marsh's Enchanted Village. The younger John has also been writing since 1991 for the *Post-Gazette*, and his column, "Nanna and Babbononno," is the depiction of the trials and tribulations of the generations of his Italian family in America. The weekly stories depict events he has experienced or stories he has heard from family elders and show a cross-section of Italian American life.

WILLIAM CONDAXIS

William Condaxis was born in raised in Manhattan, near Carnegie Hall, where his father owned a diner. The family were Greek immigrants from Turkey, and they moved to New Doorp on Staten Island, where William attended high school. He served in the navy during World War II, and after his discharge, he secured a job at Bigelow Carpet in New York. Thanks to the GI Bill and the encouragement of the owner of the company, he was accepted by Brown University and eventually graduated in 1955 after having served in the Korean War, where he served state-side in Norfolk, Virginia, calibrating ships that were to be sent to Korea.

Married in 1952 to Frances Bellantoni of Medford, who was working as a dietitian in Providence, Rhode Island, they were like most of the postwar generation, seeking stability in both home and career. In 1955, Condaxis was accepted into the Executive Training Program at Jordan Marsh. Started by Edward J. Mitton, this two-year program was begun in the late 1940s with an average of forty people in a class that worked six days a week, with assignments that were required to be completed in the evening. This cooperative type of job, a sort of Jordan Marsh MBA, studying while working to learn the operations and business profile of the company, was to eventually graduate people who were well equipped to deal with the daily operation of Boston's largest department store. The job, he said, offered a "series of things that moved employees to different departments to learn how to do the job."

After graduating from Executive Training, Condaxis was to work with Winnie Hicks, the first buyer in children's wear, in infant furniture at a fifty-dollar-per-week salary. This job entailed everything from buying the furniture and supervising the employees who sold it to going to the branch stores to oversee the departments there. He eventually worked in children's clothing. During that time, his daughter and two sons were recruited to model children's clothes for Jordan Marsh, and "they counted bras as a summer job" at the store. In 1959, two days before the Enchanted Village of Saint Nicholas was opened to the public, he and his wife took their children to see it with their Fellow Workers and their families, enjoying the holiday music and food. People came from everywhere, and "it was huge," with people waiting in long lines. By 1963, Condaxis had received a promotion to cosmetics, which he said was a big change. He was promoted to general merchandising manager and, in the early 1970s, to vice president of cosmetics and children's wear. He remained at the Boston store until 1979, when he was sent to the South Shore Plaza store in Braintree to straighten it out.

However, his abilities as a manager were obvious, and he was recruited by Metasco International, which was an overseas organization all over Europe providing trustworthy business relations among its buyers worldwide, with an office in New York. Buyers could travel the world and use Metasco's offices for help if necessary. He joined Elizabeth Arden in New York in 1980 and served as the boutique manager, traveling to the Milan and Paris fashion shows. In 1983, he moved to Mervyn's in California, serving as the manager of shoes and children's wear, but while at Mervyn's, he was posted to its office in Hong Kong for two years, where he worked with shoe buyers coming to China and gave tours of the factories, allowing them to buy shoes for their stores. After a successful career, all thanks to the Jordan Marsh Executive Training Program, he and his wife retired to Bourne, Massachusetts, in 1995; they are residents of Boston today.

William A. Eagan

William A. Eagan Jr. entered the Executive Training Program at Jordan Marsh in 1949 and, following his successful completion of the program, spent the next thirty-three years associated with New England's largest department store.

Following service in the navy during World War II, where he served on the bridge of the USS *Princeton*, an aircraft carrier, he returned to Massachusetts

In 1956, the Half Century Club inducted new members after fifty years of service to Jordan Marsh. *From left to right*: Michael E. Dwyer, new Half Century Club member; Marie Taff Mitton; Martin J. Molloy, new Half Century Club member; Edward R. Mitton, president of Jordan Marsh; Mary A. Griffin, new Half Century Club member; and James H. Fairclough, vice president of Jordan Marsh and the evening's toastmaster.

and enrolled at Holy Cross, graduating with the class of 1949. He was said by Holy Cross president Father Michael McFarland to have been "an outstanding student with a keen sense of fairness and a tremendous work ethic." As Reverend John Brooks, Holy Cross president emeritus, said of him, "Upon graduating from Holy Cross, Bill was recruited to work in a demanding and grueling business environment where the competition alone must have tempted him on occasion to wonder just how far he might advance while continuing to adhere to the lofty ethical values which were so much part of his character." That competitive environment at Jordan Marsh was to propel him after a five-year stint as a glove buyer to become a merchandising manager and later an executive vice president for merchandising.

Thanks to the Executive Training Program instituted by George W. Mitton to recruit, train and utilize the managerial skills the employees learned from this two-year program, William Eagan excelled and, for over three decades, added his expertise to the success of Jordan Marsh. After he left the company, he joined LeeJay Bed & Bath and later served as a consultant to many expanding regional stores, including the Christmas Tree Shops.

James Fisk Jr.

One of the more infamous employees of Jordan Marsh & Co. was James Fisk Jr., who was born and raised in Brattleboro, Vermont. His father was an enterprising businessman who was a fairly successful peddler, as well as the owner of the Revere House hotel on Main Street in Brattleboro, where his son worked as a waiter. After a short period, young Fisk also became a peddler who dressed in fantastic and outlandish uniforms and traveled the back roads of Vermont in a colorfully painted wagon that attracted as much attention as his attire. It was said that Fisk had "glamour, spectacle and flair," and since much of the goods he sold came from Jordan Marsh & Co. in Boston, it seems providential that this rural huckster would attract great attention with his quality goods. Eben Dyer Jordan was said to have "noticed how much merchandise the younger Fisk was selling and offered him a job in Boston. Fisk quickly accepted and moved to the city," where he became a salesman in the dry goods company.

The new job with Jordan Marsh was a great opportunity, but after his flamboyant peddling, the new job proved boring. Fisk must have felt uninspired among Jordan Marsh's countless salesmen, but he saw his chance when the Civil War broke out in 1861. He talked Eben Jordan and Benjamin Marsh into sending him to Washington, D.C., to drum up contracts to produce textiles to be made into uniforms for the Union army. "Fisk booked the best suite at the fashionable Willard's Hotel, set up an open bar and lavish buffet, and invited congressmen and military officers to talk business. Government orders came rolling in for uniforms, underwear, socks, blankets. Demand outstripped supply. Fisk wired back instructions for Jordan to buy more mills. Fisk knew he was making the company rich and asked to be made a partner. Jordan immediately agreed."

The goods James Fisk was selling the government were of good quality; however, there were inadequate supplies. The war had cut the North off from its main cotton supplier, the Southern states, and any cotton supplies to be found in the North were selling at exorbitant prices. So Fisk discharged

In 1963, nine members of the Jordan Marsh Half Century Club received checks in the amount of $1,000 for their fifty years of employment at the store. *Seated from left to right:* Mildred Harmon, Josephine Norris, Eva Bullard and Catherine Malloy; *standing from left to right:* Cameron S. Thompson, president of Jordan Marsh; Helen Gorman; Mary V. Foley; Helen C. Coughlin; Edward R. Mitton, chairman of the board of Jordan Marsh; Mary E. Sullivan; and Elizabeth M. Fogg.

agents to the South to buy massive amounts of the contraband cotton and hired shippers to sneak it through the Union blockade in any way possible. Fisk's reasons for dealing in cotton might appear to be selfless, but the contraband cotton was to help keep Northern mills operating. Fisk's wartime dealings, which also included selling Confederate bonds to European investors, made him inordinately wealthy, and he promptly parted ways with Jordan and Marsh.

Following his speculation during the Civil War, Fisk went on to become a major force on Wall Street, winning and losing huge fortunes in the market. He was considered the quintessential robber baron, as unscrupulous financiers were known during the nineteenth century. His actions caused a financial panic that led him and his partners to use bribery and stock fraud to bring about Black Friday in 1869, which ruined average investors but made him and his partners an immense fortune. His garishly salacious life led to his being murdered by no less than the new paramour of his mistress who had tried to blackmail Fisk, who could not withstand the duplicity of the two swindlers. Once so full of promise with his high-handed and flamboyant actions, his death was an ignominious end to one of Eben Jordan and Benjamin Marsh's once aspiring junior partners.

JOHN P. HICKEY

John P. Hickey (1922–2013) was the son of Thomas and Kathryn Hiss Hickey and was born in South Bend, Indiana. It was said that "at the age of five he and his brothers played football with the iconic Notre Dame football coach Knute Rockne, who was the family's next-door neighbor, and the godson of John's parents."

The invitation to John P. Hickey's surprise retirement soiree in 1987 from the Jordan Marsh store at Shoppers World in Framingham was held at the Westin Hotel and was a popular and well-attended send-off for the man who, as the invitation stated, "got the 'H' out of Framingham and the place will never be the same without him."

He attended the University of Notre Dame, class of 1944, where he was awarded in 1943 the university's Byron V. Kanaley Award for the student-athlete who has been exemplary as a student and leader. His education was interrupted, as he was to serve in the United States Navy for three years during World War II. He enrolled in the United States Navy V-12 officer-training program in July 1943, and after completing the ninety-day program, he was assigned to the Navy Supply Corps School at Wellesley College near Boston, Massachusetts. He was later appointed naval paymaster in Pearl Harbor, Hawaii, for two years. After the war, he returned to Notre Dame and completed his degree in accounting there in 1947. Following his graduation from the Harvard Business School in June 1949 with an MBA in retailing, he joined Jordan Marsh in Boston.

His first job was in the downtown offices of Jordan Marsh Company until the first branch store was opened with great fanfare on October 4, 1951, in the brand-new Shoppers World Mall in Framingham, Massachusetts. The department store's expansion to the suburbs was due to the ascendancy of the automobile, and being located on Route 9, Shoppers World was only twenty-two miles west of the city but strategically located between Boston and Worcester in the heart of the developing suburbs west of Boston. Shoppers World has the distinct honor of being the first outdoor shopping center built east of the Mississippi River. The large Jordan Marsh dome, referred to at the time of its construction as being "futuristic, flying saucer-like," was on the southern end of the mall and was the sole anchor store in the earliest years. The massive white dome was visible from the air and was actually used on aeronautical charts as a visual reporting point for aircraft approaching Boston's Logan Airport. It was reputed to be the third largest in diameter unsupported dome in the world after St. Peter's Basilica in Rome and St. Paul's Cathedral in London. The domed store was quite an architectural feat and afforded great cachet for the store.

John Hickey's first job at the Jordan Marsh store in Shoppers World was as assistant manager. He eventually assumed the general manager's job later in the decade and was to remain in that position for thirty-eight years until 1987, the year he retired as a vice president of Jordan Marsh.

CHIP HILTON

In an online reminiscence in "Shopping Days in Retro Boston," Chip Hilton provided an outline of his days at Jordan Marsh as a Fellow Worker in the 1970s. He said:

> There was a hierarchy. I was the lowest of the low for a while, an E-Con white card. That meant that not only was working contingent on staffing needs, but the white card meant you went from department to department sometimes on just a few hours notice from Mr. Skill in the Chauncy St. employment office. In this capacity you saw every Dollar Day in the Great Basement Store, where you had to ring every item up separately. So when the priest bought 40 shirts and 50 pair of socks (from the Boston Sock Exchange in the basement) I keyed 90 entries. Working the basement ingrained my fellow worker number in my head. 73658. The 7 meant you started as a white card.

Eben Dyer Jordan Jr. (1857–1916) followed his father as president of Jordan Marsh upon his death in 1895. He started his career after his graduation from Harvard College as a foreign buyer and would revolutionize the department store through innovations that Victorian Bostonians marveled at. It was said of him that he was "endowed with a wonderfully attractive and commanding personality [as well as having] the gift of winning the affection of his great army of employees and the esteem of all who met him."

You were supposed to use certain pockets in your sales book for certain parts of the three-part sales check, but most Fellow Workers put the audit copy upside down on the cover under an elastic. It was generally acceptable, but one time some big shot was roaming around and the word came to "put the audit slips inside" before he arrived. I think he was the general merchandise manager who was married to the buyer in luggage. Above it all on the sales floor were the blue leads (as in pencil lead), named for the color of the china markers they signed stuff with when you needed approval for a void, or a charge—send or something like that. They were the buyers and assistant buyers on the merchandise side, and the floor managers on the sales side. Merchandising and sales were separate organizations and one quickly learned that buyers were not always on the floor, easily avoided and with relatively little clout over sales employees. Then there were the red leads, who could sign off on some things but not all. Low level functionaries who could get their drawers balanced quickly.

Much of my time was in the annex, which we were told to refer to as the "Store for Homes." I learned to maneuver my way through the back rooms during a stint in Luggage. Best spot was first floor, store for homes, working the coffee counter, which was close to the Washington Street entrance with the bakery (ie blueberry muffin) counter on our left deeper into the store. It was the first place I ever encountered coffee snobs (they all wanted something called Hotel Blend).

EBEN DYER JORDAN

The following account of the life of Eben Dyer Jordan appeared as his obituary in the *New York Times* in 1895:

Mr. Jordan's name is familiar in the commercial centers of Europe as well as in America. He stood at the head of Boston merchants as well as at the head of the big establishment which bore his name. His career was strikingly interesting for it showed how a penniless boy can, by integrity, diligence energy and enterprise, build up a prosperous business and accumulate a fortune rated well up among the millions, while he at the same time secured an enviable position among public-spirited citizens and representative men of a great Commonwealth.... With the death of his father which occurred when Eben D. Jordan was yet a mere lad, he was left absolutely penniless and his mother, who found a large family of small children entirely dependent upon her for support was by forced of circumstances compelled to place her son Eben out in the family of a large farmer in the neighborhood, in order to enable him to earn his own living. He was a smart, quick, energetic, and remarkably industrious boy. Like all farm boys, he did the hard work in summer and the chores in winter, attending the district school during the winter months. There he received all the education he ever had, although in later life this was supplemented by a wide and exceedingly varied course of reading, and by extensive travel and intercourse with men in all parts of Europe and America....

The first chance he had was to work on a farm at West Roxbury, at the magnificent salary of $4 per month and his board, and he accepted it, trusting to fortune to open the way to something better. When he was sixteen years old he became a clerk in the dry goods store of William P Tenney & Co., where he remained for two years, subsequently entering the employ of another merchant named Pratt, where he received a salary of $275 per annum. His energy and capacity had enabled him to make a rapid advance in the estimating of his employers and had attracted the attention of others as well and when he was nineteen years old, Joshua Stetson, who was one of the leading merchants of Boston at that time, and who appreciated his ability, offered to assist him in starting a business on his own account.

This kind offer Mr. Jordan was not slow in accepting and with Mr. Stetson's assistance he secured the lease of a store at Hanover and Mechanic streets, at the North End and stocked it with a full line of the leading staples in dry goods. Enterprising, full of an energy that never tired, and determined to succeed with his new venture, he was fully alive to the possibilities of his trade. He saw that the Provincial and Portland boats landed their passengers at 4 o'clock on the morning of their arrivals, and then decided to have his store open at that hour, in order to enable the people who came from those points to utilize their time in Boston to the greatest advantage. Old-time merchants had never thought of such a thing. It was entirely unprecedented and was an innovation they could not countenance, but, nevertheless, he persisted, and had his reward, for he got all of the trade, and his store became what he desired to make it, a resort for the down-East merchant, and the down-East customer. It was there that he beat many of his competitors. He shrewdly and carefully studied the wants of his patrons and then so arranged his business as to afford the best facilities for trade in his power.

It was in the little dingy store on Hanover Street that he laid the foundation of his fortune. At the end of four years, he was doing a business that amounted to over $100,000 a year. When he was 25 years old he sold his store on Hanover Street and with the purpose of gaining a clear insight into the manner of transacting business in the best possible school, and especially with the intention of learning how to judge and to buy goods, he obtained a situation in the great dry goods house of J.M. Beebe, where he acquired not only a practical knowledge of the principles, methods and in the management of a great business enterprise, but of the system which Mr. Beebe had perfected only after 25 years of close and assiduous labor and study.

When he had wholly mastered these details he felt fully competent to begin that career, which he had continued with so much honor and profit. In 1851 the firm of Jordan, Marsh & Co was formed, the junior partner being Charles Marsh. They began a jobbing business in a small way on Milk Street. Both partners were well known in the trade and enjoyed an excellent reputation for industry, integrity and enterprise. Their trade increased and in a short time they had a large and lucrative business. Always on the alert to increase the facilities of trade and to better the methods of doing business, Mr. Jordan adopted the cash system, which was quite a change in the jobbing trade. In 1851, there were few large importers in Boston and these had established their credit abroad on a firm basis and hence enjoyed facilities in this respect that new competitors could not hope to secure. With this in mind, Mr. Jordan went abroad in 1852, and established relations with the trade, which was advantageous and the foreign correspondents never regretted.

This was another innovation which was successful from the first and has been enjoyed since by the firm. In the meantime the firm continued to prosper and the trade showed a handsome increase with the close of each year. Then came the panic of 1857, which caught many great concerns with all sails set, and left them helpless wrecks by the way when the storm was over. The firm of Jordan, Marsh & Co. successfully withstood the shock and when the trouble was passed enlarged its salesrooms, and increased its manufacturing facilities. In 1861, Jordan, Marsh & Co. found the business still prosperous and still increasing. The firm had been looking for a more suitable and convenient location for some time, and as business began to boom it bought the store at Avon and Washington Streets, which covered a part of the present location of its great establishment. The store has been enlarged by additions on the side and rear. It is the largest establishment in New England and one of the largest in the world.

Edward R. Mitton, *right*, congratulates Albert Istorico and Barbara Fraser, who in 1958 were two of the sixty-four graduating members of the Jordan Marsh Executive Training Program. This program was begun in 1919 by George W. Mitton and drew candidates primarily from within the store and trained them on a "rotation plan—from receiving room to warehouse, from credit office top sales counter, from inventory to advertising." In essence, it was a Jordan Marsh MBA.

Jordan was most entirely devoted to his business all through his life and persistently declined to accept office, even when the public demand that he should sink his personal preferences was most emphatic and pronounced. He was one of the most public-spirited men of Boston and was ever ready to help forward any project designed to secure good government, promote the best interests of all or help the suffering. When a call was made on Boston's generosity for contributions, Jordan was always one of the first to respond, not only with a liberal contribution but often with the offer of personal services to help on the good work. On the outbreak of the war, his devotion to the flag and the loyalty to the Union overcame every other consideration, and all through that long and bitter struggle he upheld the cause with a courage that never weakened in the darkest hour and a loyalty that never faltered when defeat seemed to stare the government in the face.

He was one of the prime movers in the great Peace Jubilee and then was a willing worker in the interest of the city of his adoption. He married in 1847, resided at 46 Beacon Street on Beacon Hill and was a member of the Temple Club and Trinity Church. Always faultlessly attired, he moved with a quick, elastic step and kept a constant watch on all the vast mechanism of his establishment. Eben Dyer Jordan was exceedingly democratic, always approachable and, in conversation, pleasant and agreeable.

EBEN DYER JORDAN JR.

The youngest son of Eben Dyer and Julia Clark Jordan, Eben Dyer Jordan Jr. (1857–1916) was educated at Phillips Andover and the Adams Academy in Quincy and graduated from Harvard College, class of 1880. "After leaving college he entered his father's mercantile house as a clerk, and was soon advanced to foreign buyer. In this latter position he acquired a thorough and comprehensive knowledge of the world's markets. In 1880 he was made a member of the firm, and in 1895 he became the head of the house of Jordan, Marsh & Company" upon the death of his father. His attention to business detail was paramount, but it was his artistic side that most Bostonians remember him for. He was the promoter of grand opera in Boston and was to finance the construction of a magnificent opera house in the Back Bay, designed by Wheelwright and Haven. He sponsored the organization of an opera company composed of the best artists of the world. For many years, he met the cost of the opera company and even provided the heavy velvet stage curtains from Jordan Marsh. He was also responsible for the establishment of the New England Conservatory of Music in Boston, Jordan Hall perpetuating his name, and until it was able to become self-supporting was its financial sponsor. He was also a director of the Metropolitan Opera Company of New York and an honorary director of the Royal Opera in London.

Eben Dyer Jordan Jr., like his father before him, was one of the owners of the *Boston Globe*, in which his father had invested in the 1870s to assist its founder, Charles H. Taylor. He served as a director of the Boston Dry Goods Company and a benefactor of Jordan Hospital (now known as Beth Israel Deaconess Hospital–Plymouth) in Plymouth, Massachusetts. In sporting life, according to his niece Joan Bentnick-Smith, he kept a state-of-the-art model horse stud in Plymouth and was a leading exhibitor at horse shows in Boston, New York, Chicago and Philadelphia: "In the gentlemen's classes he drove his own entries and displayed a fine quality of horsemanship."

He was lauded in *The Historical Register* as having been "endowed with a wonderfully attractive and commanding personality....Mr. Jordan had the gift of winning the affection of his great army of employees and the esteem of all who met him. The universal range of his information, the clarity and decisiveness of his views made even those who met him but casually feel that they were in the presence of a leader of men." His death in 1916 led to the appointment of George W. Mitton as president.

JAMES CLARK JORDAN

The eldest surviving son of Eben Dyer and Julia Clark Jordan, James Clark Jordan (1850–1910) was educated at the Boston Latin School and graduated from Harvard College, class of 1870. It was said in his entry in the *Harvard College Class of 1870 Secretary's Report* that since graduation from Harvard, he had been connected with the dry goods house of Jordan Marsh & Co. of Boston. Though he was with the store for eighteen years, he left in 1888, and after his subsequent divorce from Helen Lincoln Stevens Jordan, he moved to the West Coast, where he was largely interested in San Francisco and Oakland, California real estate. Today, Jordan Park in San Francisco perpetuates his name. In fact, he was said to be "one of the largest operators and believers in San Francisco real estate." He was later married to Jeannette Stiles Jordan, and though he kept a residence in Boston, as well as in San Francisco and at Pollet River in New Brunswick, he was no longer associated with the store after 1890.

TIMOTHY J. MCCARTHY

Since the late nineteenth century, Jordan Marsh had been sending buyers to Europe to secure fashionable women's and men's clothing, children's outfits and baby layettes, unique accessories and home accents, books, stationery and kitchen goods, as well as a wide assemblage of items such as china, pictures and bric-a-brac that could be sold in Boston's largest and most diverse department store.

Among the buyers who sought out the very finest accessories in Europe was Timothy McCarthy (1858–1912), who was a buyer of stationery for Jordan Marsh Company. He went to Europe in March 1912, his twenty-second trip abroad for the company, to secure fine stationery and writing papers to be offered at the store. Timothy and Mary Anastasia Haggerty McCarthy and their five children lived at 52 Nelson Street in Dorchester, a street laid out in 1885 connecting Norfolk and Selden Streets in an area that attracted aspiring middle-class residents who bought houses in the large-scale development of the newly annexed neighborhoods of Boston. He had been employed by Eben Dyer Jordan, who in 1882 had brought twenty-seven workers—such as buyers, dressmakers and style experts— in the department store on the SS *Batavia*, which duly arrived in England, where the group was received by no less than the lord mayor of London. It was said in *Retail and Romance* that the "hand of John Bright was shaken, and Victor Hugo, and President Grevy, of France. Lilian Nordica [the great opera singer from Dorchester] whose mother worked for Jordan's as a ladies' dressmaker, gave the delegation an evening reception at her apartment in Paris and sang 'divinely.' Monsieur Lafayette, grandson of the Marquis, was 'constantly with our party.' Yes indeed. Europe took considerable notice." Obviously, Jordan's "eagerness for buying abroad found chance for expression" and furthered the cachet that Jordan Marsh maintained.

McCarthy had been in London to buy stationery, but after placing his orders, his return passage was booked on the RMS *Titanic*, the new luxury liner of the White Star Line that was making its maiden voyage from Southampton, England, to New York, with stops at Cherbourg, France, and Queenstown, Ireland, along the way. The *Titanic* was said to have carried some of the wealthiest people in the world, as well as hundreds of immigrants from Great Britain, Ireland, France, Scandinavia and many other European countries seeking a new life in North America. McCarthy and Herbert H. Hilliard (1867–1912)—a fellow buyer from Jordan Marsh who lived on Hichborn Street in Brighton, Massachusetts, with his wife, Sarah Curtis Hilliard, and five children—shared First Class Cabin E-46. It was remarkable in itself that Jordan Marsh treated its buyers with such a comfortable passage. It was testimony to the high degree of respect that Jordan Marsh employees were held by both the Jordan and the Mitton families, who served as presidents of Jordan Marsh for over a century. Unfortunately, McCarthy and Hilliard's trip ended when the ship struck an iceberg and they and 1,514 other passengers, staff and crew lost their lives when the ship foundered on April 15, 1912.

BENJAMIN LLOYD MARSH

Benjamin Lloyd Marsh (1823–1865) was the son of Captain Reuben and Mary Wetherbee Marsh and was raised in Chesterfield Township, Chester, New Hampshire. His father was fairly prominent, having served as a selectman of the town for three terms and as captain of the Second Regiment Detached Militia at Portsmouth. Benjamin Marsh was an enterprising man, and his dry goods store, Marsh and Bartlett, later to be known as Marsh & Co., was located at 168 Hanover Street in Boston's North End. However, according to the *History of Cheshire and Sullivan Counties, New Hampshire*, "While a young man he went to Boston, and [later] became, in 1851, a member of the great dry-goods firm of Jordan, Marsh & Co., the senior partner of which is Eben D. Jordan. Mr. Marsh retained his connection with the firm till his death, which occurred June 13, 1865, 'Having shared in all the struggles, vicissitudes and triumphs of the house.'"

Marsh married Annie E. Smith, the eldest daughter of Samuel J.H. Smith, Esq., in 1854 at the Second Reformed Presbyterian Church at 27 Chambers Street, by the Reverend Dr. Barrett. They lived at 12 Allen Street (now Cardinal O'Connell Way) in Boston's West End. The Marshes were the parents of two daughters, Cora Marsh and Mary Louise Marsh, who died young. He died in New York City, according to the *New York Times*, and was buried at Mount Auburn Cemetery in Cambridge. His partnership in Jordan Marsh & Co. ended upon his death, though his younger brother Charles Marsh remained a junior partner until his death in 1888. Annie Smith Marsh was later remarried to Stephen R. Pearl, partner of Pearl, Smith & Co. in Boston, and they lived at 317 Beacon Street in Boston's Back Bay. Their daughter Cora Marsh Hawes, the wife of Joseph Prince Hawes Jr., lived at 398 Beacon Street and kept a house at Savin Hill in Dorchester.

CHARLES MARSH

As said in *Sketches of Successful New Hampshire Men*:

Yankee courage, integrity, and judgment have won no more substantial or more splendid triumphs in the business world than are reflected from the dry-goods palace of Jordan, Marsh, & Co., a house whose grand successes have made it famous throughout the mercantile world. The foundations of this magnificent establishment were laid in 1851 and 1852, by three young men, two of whom were natives of New Hampshire. The head of the firm, Eben D. Jordan, when fourteen years old had gone up to Boston from his home in Maine, and began his business career as an errand boy, and in a short time had been promoted to a clerkship, in which position he made himself master of the dry-goods business, and while doing it became acquainted with two other young men, Benjamin L. and Charles Marsh, who had left their father's house in Chesterfield, N.H., and sought in Boston an opening in which pluck, push, and perseverance, unaided by influential friends or unearned capital, could carry them on to success.

In 1851, Messrs. Jordan and Benjamin L. Marsh established the firm of Jordan, Marsh, & Co., and the next year Charles Marsh, then a clerk in the store of Pearl, Smith, & Co., was admitted as a partner. The house began in a small way; it had behind it little but the splendid courage and the remarkable abilities of the three young partners; but these were sufficient to win a fair share of business, and a reputation which was better than money, and in a short time it was firmly established in the confidence of the mercantile world and the good will of the public. In eight years the business had grown to two million dollars per annum, and since that time it has steadily and rapidly increased, until the firm controls the dry-goods market of New England, and, in many lines, of the entire country.

The elder Marsh died in 1865, leaving his partners to carry on and complete the grand enterprises he had helped project and begin. His brother still remains to share with Mr. Jordan the triumphs of the firm. In the early days of the business, Charles Marsh was an active salesman, and was accounted one of the best ever known in Boston. Afterwards, he took charge of the wholesale department, which has since been and still is under his personal supervision.

In commercial circles and in the store he has a clearly defined and high rank as a manager, with rare combination of talents. His coolness, his thorough knowledge of the business, his level-headed judgment, and organizing and executive capacity are abundantly attested in the great and rapid growth of the wholesale business. He is a balanced man; and how necessary this quality is to success in an enterprise of this magnitude, only those who have seen houses go to wreck for lack of it can tell. The elements of personal popularity in his character, and his extensive acquaintance throughout the country, help to explain his success. For nearly thirty years his steady hand has been felt at the helm, and yet he seems to-day only in the prime of his powers.

CONSTANCE L. MARTIN

Constance Martin is the daughter of Stephanie Martin and the late Gordon A. Martin. Born in Boston and initially educated in Brighton, she and her family moved to Newton Centre, Massachusetts, where she attended Newton Country Day School of the Sacred Heart and Newton North High School. A graduate of Harvard/Radcliffe College, in 1983, she interviewed for the Executive Training Program at Jordan Marsh, which seemed to attract young, well-educated people who might choose retail as their career.

The Executive Training Program, instituted by George Mitton in the 1920s as the first such program in the history of retail trade, was envisioned to "train its own future officers and should promote from within whenever possible." This outreach after World War II broadened its scope from within the store to college campuses throughout New England. In fact, the interview for the program took place on the Harvard campus and proved promising, as she got a call back to come for a group dinner and day of interviews in

Braintree. The dinner took place on February 28, 1983, which coincided with the last episode of the immensely popular television show *M*A*S*H*, so people joked about rushing through dinner to adjourn to the TVs in their hotel rooms. Though she attended, she said that "my heart was not set on getting the job, so didn't it prove to be one of the best interviews of my life."

During the meeting, she sat next to Elliot Stone, who happened to be the president of Jordan Marsh. Not knowing who he actually was but wanting to include him in the conversation, she said politely, "Tell me what you do at Jordan Marsh," which must have raised an eyebrow. He responded enthusiastically, describing a typical day. The next day, the candidates sat in a circle, with the Human Resource staff and store executives seated in the rear of the conference room, and they were asked what they would put in a time capsule if they were to fill it with memorabilia of 1983. The group seemed reticent to express opinions, so Constance took it upon herself to call on people to deter shyness. The choices were not important, but observing the candidates' ability to work as a group was an important part of the vetting process. The candidates were also interviewed individually, following the group exercise. Things went well, and she was offered a position in the Training Program and was assigned to the downtown Boston store (assignments were loosely based on where people lived) and started in April 1983. The Training Program, including several of the candidates she had met, began with a week of group training. Subsequently, there was usually one class every two weeks, sometimes in downtown Boston or at the Burlington or Braintree store, supplemented by on-the-job training, an important part of the program usually conducted by recent graduates of the Training Program. Training Program classes focused on analysis of merchandise trends or management techniques such as conducting performance evaluations or terminating an employee.

Constance's first assignment was in the Basement Men's Shop, a somewhat shabby area, where she reported to a department manager, a Mount Holyoke graduate, who offered instruction on arranging the merchandise and working with staff. After observing her first Dollar Day (the first Wednesday of the month when Jordan Marsh offered sales and discounts throughout its basement store), she was able to make suggestions that were implemented: additional trash cans to minimize litter and cash pickups by managers from "upstairs" to free the basement managers to get merchandise onto the sales floor.

The second assignment was a six-week assignment in Housewares with an energetic and experienced manager and visually appealing merchandise.

The third assignment was in Baby Clothes, where she finally worked with the buyer.

Within a few months, she was transferred/promoted to the Jordan Marsh at Shoppers World in Framingham and was put in charge of her own department. Her assignment was Men's Furnishings, which offered shirts, ties, handkerchiefs and cuff links. The managerial staff, she said, were often well educated, and the store often cast a "wide net, hoping people [recruited to work at Jordan Marsh] would stay." Stone often visited the stores in rotation and with advance notice; if inventory was low, the staff would need to borrow merchandise from other stores so he would see each department at its best. He was famous for asking unpredictable questions about various items, so managers were required to know their merchandise inside and out and be able to rattle off sales and style information. Once he left, everything went back to normal, and the staff or buyers would return the merchandise that had been borrowed. Retail, she said, "is not a fun business," and working in the malls required extended hours and six-day weeks, with little positive reinforcement from senior management. With modest salaries and only one Saturday off a month, the Training Program had high turnover. Traveling to Training Program classes was a welcome distraction from the grind of managing a busy department, and some of the participants developed close friendships.

Constance left after eight months to work in publishing and later obtained both an MBA and a law degree. Today, she is employed at Boston Planning and Development Agency and retains fond memories of her time at Jordan Marsh.

GEORGE W. MITTON

George Wade Mitton (1869–1947) was the son of Edward J. and Sarah Wade Mitton and started at Jordan Marsh in 1887 as a stock boy. His father had been associated with the store since 1861, so he knew it well from the time he was a child. He was married to Annie Richardson Mitton, and they lived on Corey Hill at the corner of Beacon Street and Summit Avenue in Brookline. On the death of Eben Dyer Jordan Jr. in 1916, Mitton was elected president of Jordan Marsh, and he was to maintain "the unbroken tradition of personal honesty, business integrity, keen merchandising sense, that means Jordan Marsh Company to all New England." He served as president of Jordan Marsh until 1930, when he was elected chairman of the board, a position that he held until his death.

RICHARD MITTON

Richard Mitton (1884–1945) was the son of Edward J. and Sarah Wade Mitton and was educated at Harvard University, class of 1908. He joined Jordan Marsh upon his graduation. He was married to Margaret Leonie Mitton. For two decades, he filled executive positions within the company until 1930, when he was elected president of Jordan Marsh following his brother George W. Mitton. During that time, he served as president of the Boston Retail Trade Board and was a staunch promoter of the Allied Department Stores, of which Jordan Marsh became a part and which offered larger chain store advantages. He retired from active business in 1937 and lived between his flat at the Ritz Carlton in Boston's Back Bay and his summer estate in Beach Bluff, Swampscott.

EDWARD R. MITTON

Edward Richardson Mitton (1896–1973) was the third Mitton family member to serve as president of Jordan Marsh, being preceded by his father, George W. Mitton (1916–30), and his uncle Richard Mitton (1930–37). He graduated from Milton Academy and Harvard University, class of 1919, and was married to Marie Taff Mitton. He became a salesman at Jordan Marsh in 1917 and was to serve in the United States Naval Reserve during World War I. After returning from service, he began selling in the yard goods department, later serving as floor manager and then assistant to Wilfred Tufts, general merchandising manager. Elected a director of the company in 1924, he was to become merchandising vice president in 1931.

He was elected first vice president in 1932 and the next year became a director of Hahn Department Stores, now the Allied Stores Corporation, the parent company of which Jordan Marsh became a wholly owned subsidiary in 1929. Mitton succeeded his uncle as president of Jordan Marsh in 1937, and under "his direction, the store greatly expanded, both in selling area and sales volume." He was instrumental in organizing Metasco, Inc., the foreign buying branch of Allied, and had it ready shortly

Edward Richardson Mitton, *center*, was presented in 1951 with the prestigious Tobe Award for "his distinguished contribution to American Retailing." On the left is General Robert E. Wood of Sears, Roebuck & Co., and on the right is B. Earl Puckett, chairman of the board of Allied Stores in New York. Mitton also served as president of the Retail Trade Board of Boston in 1953 and 1954.

after the end of World War II, when exports from Europe resumed. It was due to his energies that Jordan Marsh saw a large new modern addition built at Summer and Chauncy Streets, having laid the cornerstone in 1949. However, it was the Enchanted Village of Saint Nicholas that all New Englanders can thank him for, having contacted with Christian Hofmann Company in West Germany to create a village of automated figures. The Enchanted Village was a huge public relations coup, and Mitton was to receive from the Federal Republic of Germany the Cross of Merit First Class and from the City of Coburg, West Germany, a testimonial for bringing the village to the children of New England.

Edward R. Mitton was awarded the Tobe Award for distinguished retailing, the Order du Merite Commercial from France and was named a Chevalier de la Legion d' Honneur. In 1962, he became chairman of the board. He was named director emeritus of Jordan Marsh and Allied Stores in 1968.

ALICE DICK MORAN

Alice Moran was born and raised in Chelsea, Massachusetts, and attended Chelsea High School. She left high school prior to graduation and was employed at the W.T. Cardy and Sons Company in Chelsea, where she made cardboard boxes for Candy Cupboard Candy, among other well-known manufacturers of chocolate.

She was to help raise her siblings after their mother's early death and would secure a position as a switchboard operator at Jordan Marsh Company, working the 3:00 to 9:00 p.m. shift, which allowed her to wait for her youngest sister to return home from school and for her husband, John Moran, to return home after work. The switchboard room was literally a wall of connections that allowed her as an operator to connect people within the store as well as incoming and outgoing calls. Located on the seventh floor, behind the Furniture Department, it was a self-contained office staffed by women who seemed to work in unison and considered this their "second home," as she said. After eight years of pleasant work, the store updated its switchboard operation to Contrex, which is a secure web-based portal that provides instant access to the system's capabilities. This new system effectively phased out the switchboard operators and also moved the office to Commander Shea Boulevard in Quincy, located in the Squantum Jordan Marsh Warehouse. Moran could not commute to the new location and retired with good memories of friendly co-workers at Jordan Marsh.

Alice Dick Moran is seen in front of the Jordan Marsh switchboard, which literally covered the entire wall of the switchboard office. It was described as a telecommunications system used in the public switched telephone network or in enterprises to interconnect circuits of telephones to establish telephone calls between the subscribers or users or between other exchanges. When someone called the store at HUbbard 2-2700, she would put the caller through to one of the many departments in the various buildings. One wonders how she did it with so many wires to connect.

Louisa Bareiss Pray

Few people have the honor of being the first customer of a newly opened business, but Louisa Bareiss was Eben Dyer Jordan's first customer when he opened his small dry goods store at the corner of Hanover Street and Mechanics Lane in Boston's North End in 1841. Her purchase of a yard of cherry-colored ribbon would be immortalized in *Tales of the Observer*. It said, "Louisa somehow had persuaded her parents to let her hurry down to Eben Jordan's new store that frosty morning in order to be his first customer. And Eben found her there waiting, shivering in the cold darkness, when he arrived to slip the lock." Many years later, at the age of ninety-three as an honored guest at the banquet of the Quarter Century Club of Fellow Workers at Jordan Marsh, Louisa Bareiss Pray proudly told of that yard of cherry-colored ribbon purchased in 1841 "and a later wedding dress purchased from Jordan's and beamed pridefully over her friend Eben's subsequent greatness."

John Pupek

As Andrea Estes said in the *Boston Globe* on December 27, 2004:

> *For decades, any decent downtown shopping trip ended at Jordan Marsh, where the promise of a sugar-crusted blueberry muffin could make annoying children angelic. Baker John Pupek followed the secret recipe one batch at a time, folding in the berries by hand to keep them whole and working the batter until the consistency felt just right.*
>
> *Pupek opened his own shop after Jordan Marsh closed its bakeries and Macy's bought the department store in the mid-1990s. His Jordan Marsh Muffin Co. in Brockton has turned out thousands of blueberry muffins a week, as well as other delicacies made famous by Jordan Marsh, since 1998. But on Christmas Eve, the muffin-maker closed his store. The iconic muffins, like Jordan Marsh itself, will become a fading memory. "We'll replace them with something else, but it will never be the same. It's the end of an era—like when they stopped making Oldsmobile's," said Morton Glovin, who sells the muffins that he savored in childhood at his two Boston Coffee Exchange locations.*
>
> *Exhausted by days that start at 2:00 AM and don't end until well into the afternoon, Pupek, 62, notified his customers and suppliers earlier*

"The Jordan Marsh Observer" was a fictional character replete with a three-cornered hat, a long clay pipe and a brass telescope who told the story of Jordan Marsh in the third person in the popular book *Tales of the Observer* by Richard H. Edwards Jr. Prescott W. Baston of Sebastian Miniatures in Marblehead, Massachusetts, produced these small ceramic figures of the Observer that, in 1951, the centennial year of the store, became a popular collectible. In 1958, a similar figurine was produced by Sebastian Miniatures to commemorate the opening of the Northshore Shopping Center.

this month that "it is time to hang up the apron and shut off the mixer and oven." He wants to relax after decades of taxing physical labor and surgery on both hands for carpal tunnel syndrome that developed after years of plopping blueberries into batter. "I love what I do, but it's very labor intensive," said Pupek, who began baking at Jordan Marsh in 1961. "The back, the feet, and the arms—I have to start relaxing the body and enjoy life right now. I don't want to be here 24/7."

The shop closed this past Friday night; the wholesale operation, which sells to small shops and restaurants around the region, will close this Friday. Pupek said he will travel, and maybe get a job driving a limousine. His daughter, Christine, his partner since the shop opened, is not interested in taking over the business—she wants to spend more time at home with her children, he said. In an age of mass production, Pupek's approach is as nostalgic as the muffins themselves. He has routinely delivered muffins to retail customers' homes, dropping them on their doorsteps at 4:00 AM. Since the letter went out, panicky customers have been stockpiling their favorites, figuring they can freeze them, give them as holiday gifts, or simply gorge. "When I got that note last Wednesday, I stood in my coffee bar and said this is an absolutely traumatic day for me," said Glovin.

Recently, at Pupek's shop, a Milton man bought 33 dozen almond macaroons; another customer ordered six dozen muffins and piles of brownies, also a Jordan Marsh specialty. The customers waxed nostalgic, Pupek said, tearfully thanking him for the confections, particularly the muffins, which evoke emotional responses even from out-of-towners.... "Nobody could make them as good as Jordan's. It was a love affair. I lived with six or seven roommates and [the muffins] *seemed so huge, we'd cut them in half. They had that incredible sugar crunchy coating on the top. The blueberries were so soft and fresh—you felt like the guy just went out and picked them,"* she said. *After this month, aficionados of the Jordan Marsh muffins will have few options. The only place that will sell them is Macy's in Portland, Maine, where Pupek's former co-worker leases the bakery and bakes muffins from frozen batter that Pupek sells her. He said he will continue to make her batter from time to time. But he said he will never sell the Jordan Marsh muffin name, which he said people now identify with him.*

"People want me to show somebody else how to make the muffins," said *Pupek, "but I can look at a finished muffin and know who made it. It's in the feel and the eye. I'll show them how to make muffins, but I won't put my name on it. That name is me.*

"If people said they had a Jordan Marsh muffin and it was horrible, it would kill me."

OLGA SEARS

Olga Itasca Sears (1906–1990) was a well-known member of the Rockport Art Association and a frequent exhibitor of her paintings. She was the daughter of Ignatius and Mary Sears and was raised in Framingham, Massachusetts, where she attended local public schools. She would later enroll in the New England School of Design, from which she graduated in 1928. She was to begin her artistic career at the Pinkham Press in Boston as a silkscreen artist, and she also worked as a life model for portrait and sculpture classes at the School of the Museum of Fine Arts while attending night classes at the school.

From 1931 to 1939, Olga Sears was a Fellow Worker of Jordan Marsh Company and worked as a display artist and assistant in the Interior Decorating Department. Art exhibits of local artists' work at Jordan Marsh had been held since the turn of the century, and after Richard Mitton became president of the store, he established the Richard Mitton Memorial Award, presented annually since 1930 to a contemporary New England artist whose work was chosen as the best of exhibition, with a cash award and a medal that would be presented at a luncheon at the Locke-Ober Restaurant in Boston. It was during this time that Sears started designing a line of Christmas cards for private customers and created woodblock prints for a photo and card shop in Hyannis on Cape Cod. In April 1939, she was thought of as a promising artist and was tutored by Charles H. Woodbury with private lessons at his art studio on the Riverway in Boston's Fenway. Later that fall, she secured the position of teaching art at Dana Hall School and Pine Manor School (later Pine Manor Junior College). The following summer she spent on Monhegan Island, a popular artist colony off the coast of Maine, where she studied with Margaret Jordan Patterson.

With a good reputation as an artist, she later taught art at St. Mary's in the Mountains in Littleton, New Hampshire, a co-educational, independent boarding school, and in the summer months at the School of the Museum of Fine Arts in Boston. In 1949, she was hired to teach art at the Vesper George School of Art Inc. in Boston, which had been founded in 1924 by Vesper Lincoln George. It was not just in the teaching art but also studying with others, among them the noted artist George Demetrios in Gloucester, that she was to hone and perfect her artistic talents. In addition to Vesper George, Olga Sears also taught art at the Boston Center for Adult Education.

Elliot Stone

Elliot J. Stone (1922–2014) was the son of Maurice and Ann Stone of Brookline, Massachusetts. He attended Brookline High School and graduated from Clark University. He began his career in retailing after having served in World War II with the 101st Airborne Division. In 1945, he entered the executive training program of R.H. White, the downtown Boston department store, where he was a buyer in the boys' wear department for six years.

In 1952, Elliot Stone moved to Pittsburgh after being hired by Gimbel Brothers, and he spent eighteen years there before taking a job with Maas Brothers stores in Tampa, Florida, where he worked for several years. In 1972, Jordan Marsh recruited him to become executive vice president for merchandising and sales; however, three years later, Gimbel Brothers hired him away from Jordan Marsh. He was named president and chief operating officer of the department store giant and returned to Pittsburgh. Four years later, Jordan Marsh's owners, Allied Stores Corporation, convinced him to return to Boston as head of the New England chain.

While at the helm of Jordan Marsh, Stone was described as an imaginative and innovative marketer, and he began to market the chain as a clothing store for working women. He closed Jordan Marsh's appliances division and custom upholstery services, two underperforming departments, to focus on women's wear. In 1981, he discussed improvement efforts at the Boston store and the challenges of bringing suburban shoppers back to downtown Boston. In 1988, he launched a two-week cultural promotion known as "The Land of Israel," featuring Israeli-made goods, live performances and exhibits. The event was part of a trade agreement Massachusetts leaders had with Israel.

Elliot Stone also oversaw a Jordan Marsh campaign in 1982 promoting goods from China, which was dubbed the "Orient Express'd," and he visited China with a group of retail executives. He spent more than four decades in retail management, including four years as president and chief operating officer of Gimbels stores. When Elliot Stone retired as president and chief executive in 1988, retail analysts sensed the end of an era. "Jordan Marsh was Mr. Stone, and vice versa," the publisher of the *Retail Marketing Report* told the *Boston Globe* at the time.

CHAPTER 9

EXHIBITS, CLUBS AND MARKETING EFFORTS

The Store with You in Mind

*J*ordan Marsh sponsored a few clubs for young girls and boys that were remarkably popular. In fact, some of them had literally thousands of members. These clubs had corresponding departments at Jordan Marsh, including Connie Cut-Ups, the Jack and Judy Jordan Shop, the Marsha Jordan Shop and the Jimmy and Johnny Jordan Shop, all on the fourth floor of the Main Store.

CONNIE CUT-UP CLUB

This club was for girls ages seven to twelve, and all were eager to join the annual contest to find the typical "pigtailer of the year." In 1947, the winner of the Connie Cut-Up Contest was Pattie Marshall of Woburn, Massachusetts. "She's a typical '7 to 14 'er' with eyes that sparkle wide and winningly and hair that pulls into pigtails or falls to cunning curls. She's 8 years old and on the Honor Roll in School. You'll like her as we do....Be seeing her in our newspaper announcements...in the Connie Cut-up Shop...and if you're a member of the Connie Cut-up Club you'll be hearing from her via our Mail Newscasts." The contest judges were Francis Hart of Promotions, Inc., Joanne Daly of the Norcross School in Boston and Arlo Born, executive director of the Boston Council of Girl Scouts.

Jan Jordan Club

This club was for girls ages twelve to thirteen who wore a "pre-teen dress size 6–14." They served as a twenty-member fashion board at Jordan Marsh. The premise was that the fashion board participated in monthly board meetings on fashion and current trends in the Young Reflections Shop at the Boston Jordan Marsh, taking field trips and participating in fashion shows throughout the year. This was a contest for girls who attended public, private or parochial schools within easy commuting distance of Boston, and the requirements were that the contestants not be associated with a professional modeling agency nor be related to a Jordan Marsh employee.

This contest would elect "Jan Jordan," who would receive a $150 back-to-school wardrobe and a chaperoned trip to New York, and her fellow nineteen fashion board members would each receive a $25 back-to-school outfit. The Jan Jordan Talent Contest in 1955 elected Betty Ann Mulroy of Wellesley Hills, Massachusetts. The runners-up were Jean Vallati of Dorchester, Linda Parmenter of Hudson, Susan Capone of Malden and Linda Wainwright of East Boston. Jordan Marsh held a Jan Jordan Back-to-School Party in the Young Reflections Shop on the fifth floor of the Annex so that girls and their friends could get tickets to meet the new Jan Jordan and her new Junior High Fashion Board and join in the fun.

Marsha Jordan Club

This club was for teenage girls ages fourteen to seventeen, to be chosen from among their five-thousand-plus members once each year. They were required in writing to be "Dress size 5 to 11." Most of these young ladies had once been either Connie Cut-Up or Jan Jordan or a member of the fashion board, so they knew that their suggestions for the latest fashion trends and styles would be seriously considered by the buyers for the Young Reflection Club. From modeling at fashion shows, mother-daughter teas and conducting surveys at the store and their schools on fashion, it was cool to be a Marsha Jordan girl. In 1942, the new Marsha Jordan was Betty Ann Owens of Belmont, Massachusetts, who was elected as official sponsor of Jordan Marsh's Teen Age Shop, with runners-up Jane Evans of Scituate and Betty Ahearne of Dorchester. The contestants "were chosen for their poise, personality, good voice, ability to wear clothes well, and their ideas on back-to-school clothing." It was said in a newspaper press release that "practicality ruled the selection of the teen age clothes modeled for yesterday's capacity audience, which overflowed Jordan's New Fashion Center on the fifth floor annex, but that didn't make the ensembles any less popular, judging by the rapturous ah's and oh's which greeted many of the wardrobe pieces." The Marsha Jordan Shop was on the fourth floor of the Main Store.

WOMEN WHO WORK CLUB

Women Who Work was a group of women from eighteen Boston-based organizations who attended lectures at Jordan Marsh on styles and charm, seminars, fashion shows and other useful "networking" through the department store in the mid-twentieth century.

Beginning in 1942, this group of "Women Who Work" was composed of a group of women from eighteen Boston-based organizations who attended lectures at Jordan Marsh on style and charm, seminars, fashion shows and other useful "networking" through the department store in the mid-twentieth century. To commemorate the group, Jordan Marsh had a commemorative piece made that was a Peace silver dollar, set in a Lucite disk; it has become a highly sought-after Jordan Marsh collectible.

THE BABE RUTH JORDAN MARSH BOYS CLUB

The Babe Ruth Boys Club was a popular club for young boys who idolized the great baseball player. Jordan Marsh had the Pilgrim Badge and Specialty Company of Boston produce pins that had the face of Babe Ruth on it after he was traded to the Boston Braves in 1935. Babe Ruth, born George Herman Ruth Jr., was a beloved baseball player affectionately known as "the Bambino" or simply "the Babe." His career included the Boston Red Sox (1914–19) the New York Yankees (1920–34) and eventually the Boston Braves (1935). His return to Boston was heralded with excitement, and Richard Cressey of Medford presented on behalf of thousands of fellow members of the club a floral tribute to Babe Ruth at Braves Field. Babe Ruth is regarded as one of the greatest sports heroes in American culture and is considered by many to be the greatest baseball player of all time. In 1936, Ruth was elected into the Baseball Hall of Fame as one of its "first five" inaugural members.

There were also many well-known exhibits in the Annex that were mounted in commemoration of such things as the centennial of the Civil War, a Revolutionary War exhibit and a popular circus.

The Jordan Marsh Civil War Centennial Exhibit

This exhibit was held from June 30, 1961, to July 30, 1961. The author is indebted to Helen Hannon for the research on the Civil War Centennial Exhibit.

The centennial of the American Civil War took place from 1961 to 1965 and inspired programs and events all over the country. In 1961, Harvard University's Widener Library presented an exhibit "A Centenary Commemoration of the Beginning of the Civil War." The Boston Public Library had displays from its collection. Jordan Marsh's popular flagship store in downtown Boston also sponsored a major month-long exhibit. The location meant good crowds, and the official attendance was 148,903. Set up in the Fashion Center of the Main Store, the free exhibit included a mix of historical artifacts and accurate reproductions. The Fashion Center, a large hall on the seventh floor of the main building, was often used for a variety of programs. The most well known was a large Christmas display held every year called the Enchanted Village.

The centerpiece of the Civil War exhibit was a reproduction of the seated Lincoln statue by Daniel Chester French from the Lincoln Memorial in Washington, D.C. The reproduction statue was fifteen feet high, slightly smaller than the original, and placed on a platform. Directly behind the statue was a temple-like façade of classical columns. Ferns and a backdrop of drapes were added as additional decoration around the Lincoln statue. The display was described as "simulated marble" and was most likely fiberglass. The Lincoln arrangement was made locally by the Tirone Studios, and the artists who created it were George Tirone, Luigi Mucci and Joseph Bertucci. The Tirone studio burned down in the 1970s, and it is assumed the molds were lost at that time. Another artist, Charles Young, did a mural of the First Battle of Bull Run. The various flags used

The 100th anniversary of Jordan Marsh (1851–1951) was a great celebration throughout New England. Seen here with a two-story colored neon-lighted sign at the corner of Chauncy and Summer Streets, it proudly proclaims the anniversary of New England's greatest department store.

in the exhibit were a mix of originals and reproductions. Patriotic banners were placed around the walls. At the top of banners were canton squares of blue with a circle of white stars. Attached and placed directly below the canton was striped red, white and red cloth, bound into a rosette at the bottom to make a V. Flags showing brigade and corps designations were placed on poles jutting out from the pillars in the hall. On the walls, circling the exhibit area, large plaques, about twenty feet from the floor, showed the name of every major battle.

A large variety of displays was set up. Some were on the street-level store windows as well as the main exhibit. In the Fashion Center, there were panels at various angles; others were tiered tables against the walls holding artifacts. In the exhibit were a cannon, cannonballs, rifles, pistols, drums, sabers, torpedoes, uniforms and more. Authentic and reproduction uniforms, some on mannequins, representing both Union and Confederate soldiers were used. One uniform belonged to General William Tecumseh Sherman. There was a chair used by Robert E. Lee when he was at Gettysburg. Additional displays came from the Frank Hayes Civil War collection and artifacts from Boston's historic Association of the First Corps of Cadets, authorized by Herbert W. Frank.

The Massachusetts State Archives lent newspapers, letters and other documents from the era. Among them was the telegram sent by President Lincoln to Massachusetts governor John Andrew requesting troops. Many documents were framed and placed on the walls. There was a complete listing of all the Massachusetts regiments and the battles where they fought. The United States Navy displayed ship models, equipment, photographs and paintings of naval battles. There were photographs from the Mathew Brady studio that visually chronicled the Civil War. A reproduction of a photographer's wagon was loaned by ANSCO, a company that made photographic film and cameras. Key people connected to the exhibit were Sheriff Charles W. Hedges, chairman, and Mary D'Arcy, executive secretary of the Massachusetts Civil War Centennial Commission. From Jordan Marsh there was Cameron S. Thompson, executive vice president; E.B. Lawrence, advertising and publicity director; Walter V. Krysto, display director; and Robert Tonkin, assistant display director. Dr. Robert Hale, archivist for the commonwealth, and Professor George Blackwood, whose affiliation is unknown, were also involved with the centennial activities.

Visitors could press buttons on an interactive electrical map showing the locations of the major battles. There was also a detailed diorama of Fort Sumter. Three women—Helen Wick, Bobbie Miner and Veva Godin—were featured in newspaper articles as they worked on the dioramas. ESSO, now EXXON, gave out folding maps of battle sites. Jordan Marsh presented a thoughtful and historically accurate exhibit consistent with its quality standards. It gave many visitors an introduction to an important time in American history.

THE JORDAN MARSH CIRCUS

According to Wikipedia, "A circus is a company of performers who put on diverse entertainment shows that include clowns, acrobats, trained animals, trapeze acts, musicians, dancers, hoopers, tightrope walkers, jugglers, magicians, unicyclists, as well as other object manipulation and stunt-oriented artists. The term 'circus' also describes the performance which has followed various formats through its 250-year modern history." Jordan Marsh had been immensely successful in having Christian Hofmann

Company in West Germany produce figures and animals for the Enchanted Village of Saint Nicholas, so in the mid-1960s, Edward R. Mitton decided to have an automated circus in the Annex.

The circus had clowns that welcomed the visitors, as well as circular fence-enclosed platforms on which were a variety of circus scenes that were led by the ringleader and included lion tamers, elephants doing tricks, an ostrich, a giraffe, prancing ponies and a life-sized bear riding a unicycle. All of these tableaux were automated, and as the platforms gently turned, the automated figures and animals seemingly came to life as the people watched. It was a fun way to spend an hour, as the Jordan Marsh Circus was not only popular but also extremely well attended.

CHAPTER 10

A Few Favorite Recipes from the Jordan Marsh Bakery

The Jordan Marsh Bakery, which was located on the ground floor of the Annex Building with large plate-glass windows looking onto Washington Street, was a place where many Bostonians stopped on their way home from shopping in town for a box of pastry that often included the store's famous blueberry muffins. These muffins were so large that only six could fit in one white box, which was secured with red-and-white string. There always seemed to be a line, and after getting a numbered ticket, one waited patiently to be served by one of the women who worked behind the glass showcases filled with delights.

The Jordan Marsh Bakery

famous for its ·
delicious blueberry muffins

Has An Opportunity For

EXPERIENCED BAKER

and BAKER APPRENTICE

For its night shift 11 p.m.-7 a.m. Liberal fringe benefits including store discount after only 2 weeks employment.

Please apply Employment Office Monday thru Saturday, 9:00 A.M. to 5:00 P.M.

JORDAN MARSH

38 Chauncy Street, Boston

An Equal Opportunity Employer

A newspaper advertisement in the *Boston Globe* had an opportunity at Jordan Marsh for an experienced baker for its night shift operation. As the ad clearly stated, "The Jordan Marsh Bakery [was] famous for its delicious blueberry muffins"—as if anyone in New England was unaware of the famous muffins. This was a highly coveted position, as it not only had liberal fringe benefits but also included a store discount after only two weeks' employment.

Among the Jordan Marsh recipes were:

Jordan Marsh Blueberry Muffins

The following is said to be the authentic recipe for Jordan Marsh Blueberry Muffins used by John Pupek, from an article in the *Boston Herald*.

½ cup butter (my opinion is that Jordan's used shortening)
1 cup granulated sugar
½ teaspoon salt
2 teaspoons baking powder
2 eggs
2 cups all-purpose flour
½ cup milk
1 teaspoon vanilla
1 pint blueberries, cleaned and rinsed
Crystallized sugar, for sprinkling on top of muffins

Cream together the butter, sugar and salt for approximately 3 minutes. Add baking powder and eggs and mix well. Add flour, milk and vanilla, and mix well again. Fold in blueberries. Preheat oven to 450 degrees.

Grease and flour a 12-cup muffin pan. Fill muffin cups to the top. Sprinkle a pinch of crystallized sugar on each muffin. Bake at 450 degrees for 5 minutes, drop temperature to 375 and bake an additional 30 to 35 minutes, until golden brown. Cool and remove from pans. Makes one dozen muffins.

Notes: One can use butter, all vegetable shortening, all margarine or a blend of all. The batter will be very heavy, but be sure to fill the cups to the top of pan. When greasing pan, make sure you grease the top surface, as this will help the muffins peak into a mushroom effect. The muffins will stick if the top is not greased.

Jordan Marsh Blueberry Muffins

This is another variation of the famous blueberry muffins.

½ cup butter, softened
1 ¼ cups sugar
2 eggs
2 cups flour
½ cup sifted cake flour
½ teaspoon salt
2 teaspoons baking powder
½ cup milk
2 cups blueberries

Preheat oven to 350 degrees.

Cream the butter and sugar until light and smooth. Add the eggs, one at a time, beating well after each addition. Sift together both kinds of flour, salt and baking powder and add to the creamed mixture alternately with the milk. Crush ½ cup of the blueberries with a fork and mix into the batter. Gently fold in the remaining whole berries.

Grease 12 large muffin cups, including the surface of the tin (alternative: grease surface of tin and line tin with paper liners). Fill generously with batter. Sprinkle crystallized sugar over the tops of the muffins and bake at 350 degrees for 30 minutes, or until toothpick comes out clean.

Jordan Marsh Blueberry Loaf Cake

½ cup butter, softened
1 ¼ cups sugar
2 eggs
1 teaspoon vanilla
½ cup milk
2 cups flour
½ cup sifted cake flour
½ teaspoon salt
2 teaspoons baking powder
2 cups blueberries

Preheat oven to 375 degrees. Spray an 8x8 inch or a 9x13 inch pan with cooking spray.

Cream the butter and sugar on low until fluffy. Beat in the eggs one at a time until incorporated. Add vanilla to milk.

Mix all dry ingredients together except additional sugar used to top cake. Alternate adding dry ingredients and wet ingredients until all is mixed.

Fold in blueberries. Use fresh blueberries when available, but frozen are fine. Just add frozen berries to mix. Spread out in pan and sprinkle additional sugar on top of cake. Bake for 30 minutes if you are making muffins or 45 minutes if you are making the cake. A toothpick should come out clean when done and top will be golden. Cool completely before cutting.

Lemon Tea Loaf

3 cups sifted flour
¾ cup sugar
3 teaspoons baking power
1 teaspoon salt
¼ teaspoon baking soda
¼ teaspoon nutmeg
½ cup chopped walnuts
¼ cup firmly packed brown sugar
1 teaspoon grated lemon rind
1 egg
1¼ cups milk
4 teaspoons melted unsalted butter
1 teaspoon sugar (for topping)
1 tablespoon lemon juice (for topping)

Sift first six ingredients together in a large bowl. Stir in chopped walnuts, brown sugar and lemon rind. Beat egg with milk in a small bowl; stir in melted butter. Pour all at once into the dry mixture, and beat until evenly moistened. Spoon into a well-greased loaf pan and let set for 20 minutes. Bake in a preheated 350-degree oven for 75 minutes. Cool on a rack for 5 minutes and then loosen edges and invert on rack to cool.

Mix 1 tablespoon each of sugar and lemon juice in a cup and then brush on top of the tea loaf to glaze. Cool completely and then wrap and store for at least a day before serving.

The Food Shop and Bakery was on the ground floor of the Annex. Seen here in 1965 festively decorated for the holiday season, hundreds of people would peruse the bakery with its famous blueberry muffins and many other equally well-known items, as well as the Food Shop, where gourmet foods were available along with gift baskets that could be made up and then sent for special occasions.

Wellesley Fudge Cake

4 1-ounce squares unsweetened Baker's Chocolate
½ cup hot water
½ cup sugar
2 cups cake flour
1 teaspoon baking soda
1 teaspoon salt
½ cup unsalted butter
1 ¼ cups sugar
3 eggs
1 teaspoon vanilla
⅔ cup milk

Combine chocolate and water in the top of a double boiler and cook over hot water until chocolate melts. Add ½ cup sugar and cook 2 minutes longer. Sift flour, baking soda and salt three times. Cream the butter and then add 1¼ cups sugar and cream until light and fluffy. Add eggs one at a time, beating thoroughly after each addition. Add the vanilla and then flour alternating with the milk. Beat well after each addition, and then add the chocolate mixture and blend well. Pour batter into two well-greased 9x9 pans and bake in a preheated 350-degree oven for 20 to 30 minutes.

Macaroons

Known as Nusshaufchen, these almond macaroons were introduced to the Jordan Marsh Bakery in 1959 with the opening of the Enchanted Village of Saint Nicholas.
Makes about 3 dozen cookies

4 egg whites
1½ cups sugar
2 teaspoons lemon juice
1¼ cups finely grated almonds
1 teaspoon cinnamon
¼ teaspoon ground cloves
Pinch salt

Beat the egg whites until stiff but not dry. Fold in the sugar and add the lemon juice, finely grated almonds, cinnamon, cloves and salt. Mix thoroughly and drop batter by teaspoon-sized rounds on greased baking sheets. Let the cookies stand for 2 hours, then bake in a preheated oven at 350 degrees for 15 minutes. Loosen the cookies with a spatula, placing the cookies on a wire rack to cool completely.

Old-Fashioned Brownies

2 1-ounce squares unsweetened Baker's Chocolate
⅓ cup butter
2 eggs
1 cup sugar

½ cup sifted flour
Dash of salt
1 teaspoon vanilla
1 cup walnuts

Melt the chocolate and then add the butter. Beat the eggs well and then add 1 cup of sugar. Mix in flour, salt and vanilla until your mixture is really gooey. Spread brownie mixture evenly in an 8x10 pan. Add your walnuts to the mixture or place them on top of your brownies in the pan. Bake your Old-Fashioned Brownies at 350 degrees for 25 minutes or 325 degrees for 30 minutes. Let your brownies cool before serving.

Jordan Marsh Cranberry Muffins with Pecan Streusel Topping

Muffins
6 tablespoons unsalted butter, melted
¾ cup granulated sugar
2 eggs
1 cup buttermilk
2 cups flour
2½ teaspoons baking powder
1 teaspoon salt
½ teaspoon fresh nutmeg
½ teaspoon cinnamon
½ teaspoon ground ginger
1 teaspoon vanilla extract
Zest from one medium-size orange
1½ cups cranberries

Streusel
¼ cup flour
3 tablespoons butter, melted
¼ cup brown sugar
¾ cup pecans, roughly chopped
½ cup cranberries, halved
½ teaspoon cinnamon

For the muffins: Preheat oven to 375. Butter a 12-cup nonstick muffin tin or place a muffin liner in each cup. With a mixer on low speed, cream together the butter and sugar until light and fluffy. Add one egg at a time and mix until just combined. Then, pour in the buttermilk and the dry ingredients with the vanilla and orange zest and mix until just combined.

In a small bowl, mash ½ cup of the cranberries until pulpy and juicy. Stir these into the batter. Then, stir in the remaining whole cranberries until just incorporated. Fill each muffin cup ¾ full. Top each muffin with an equal amount of streusel filling (see below) and bake for 25 to 30 minutes.

For the streusel: In a small bowl, combine the flour, butter and sugar. Work it with your hands until everything is easily mixed and large crumbs form. Stir in the pecans, cranberries and cinnamon and set aside.

Jordan Marsh Chocolate Chip Cookies

2½ cups blended oatmeal
1 cup unsalted butter
1 cup brown sugar
1 cup sugar
2 eggs
1 teaspoon pure vanilla
2 cups flour
½ teaspoon salt
1 teaspoon baking powder
1 teaspoon baking soda
12 ounces chocolate chips
4 ounces sweet chocolate, chopped
1½ cups chopped nuts of your choice

Measure oatmeal and blend in a blender to a fine powder. Cream the butter and both sugars.

Add eggs and vanilla, mix together with flour, oatmeal, salt, baking powder and baking soda. Add chocolate chips, sweet chocolate and nuts. Scoop with tablespoon. Roll into balls and place two inches apart on a cookie sheet.

Bake in a preheated 375-degree oven for 10 minutes. Do not overbake.

Oatmeal Raisin Cookies

⅔ cup granulated sugar
⅔ cup packed brown sugar
½ cup butter softened
½ cup shortening
1 teaspoon baking soda
1 teaspoon ground cinnamon
1 teaspoon vanilla
½ teaspoon baking powder
½ teaspoon salt
2 eggs
3 cups quick-cooking or old-fashioned oats
1 cup all-purpose flour
1 cup raisins

Heat oven to 375 degrees Fahrenheit.

In large bowl, beat all ingredients except oats, flour and raisins with electric mixer on medium speed, or mix with spoon. Stir in oats, flour and raisins. On an ungreased cookie sheet, drop dough by rounded tablespoonfuls about 2 inches apart.

Bake 9 to 11 minutes or until light brown. Immediately remove from cookie sheet to cooling rack.

Molasses Cookies

¾ cup shortening
1 cup sugar
¼ cup dark molasses
1 egg
2 teaspoons baking soda
2 cups sifted all-purpose flour
1 teaspoon ground cloves
1 teaspoon ground ginger
1 teaspoon cinnamon
½ teaspoon salt

Melt shortening in a saucepan over low heat and then allow it to cool. Add sugar, molasses and the egg and beat well. Sift dry ingredients and add to first mixture, mixing well. Chill the dough 1 hour and then form the dough into 1-inch balls. Roll the balls in granulated sugar and place on a greased cookie sheet 2 inches apart. Bake in a preheated 375-degree oven for 8 to 10 minutes.

Cool on a wire rack.

Anise Cookies
These cookies were introduced to the Jordan Marsh Bakery in 1959 with the opening of the Enchanted Village of Saint Nicholas.
Makes 3 dozen cookies

8 egg whites
3 cups sugar
2¼ cups flour
1 tablespoon crushed anise seeds

Heat gently to lukewarm the egg whites and the sugar, then beat until frothy. Add the flour and the anise seeds and mix gently, putting the batter in a pastry bag. Form round cookies on a greased cookie sheet, 1 inch apart. Let them stand 2 hours and then bake in a 350-degree preheated oven for 8 to 10 minutes.

Cool on a wire rack.

Oatmeal Muffins with Raisins, Dates and Walnuts
Makes 12 muffins

1 cup rolled oats
½ cup all-purpose flour
½ cup whole wheat flour
½ cup brown sugar, packed
½ teaspoon salt
½ teaspoon baking soda
1 teaspoon baking powder
½ teaspoon cinnamon
⅓ cup finely chopped walnuts, toasted

⅓ cup chopped dates
⅓ cup golden raisins
1 cup buttermilk
1 large egg
½ teaspoon vanilla extract
1 stick unsalted butter (½ cup), melted and cooled

Preheat oven to 400 degrees Fahrenheit. Grease a muffin tin or line the slots with paper baking cups. You will need space for 12 muffins. In a large bowl, mix together the rolled oats, flour, brown sugar, salt, baking soda, baking powder, cinnamon, walnuts, dates and raisins. In a separate medium bowl, mix together the buttermilk, egg, vanilla extract and butter.

Pour the wet mixture into the dry ingredients and stir together with a spatula or wooden spoon. Stir just until combined (10 to 15 seconds); if you over-stir the batter, the muffins will become tough. Scoop the batter into your prepared muffin tin(s) and bake for about 20 minutes, or until a toothpick inserted into the center comes out clean. Cool in tins for just a moment or two, then invert onto a wire rack and cool completely.

Old-Fashioned Cherry Pie

This was a favorite of the Observer, who narrated the centennial history of Jordan Marsh in the book *Tales of the Observer*, which was written by Richard H. Edwards Jr.

Pastry

2 cups all-purpose flour
1 teaspoon salt
⅔ cup plus 2 tablespoons shortening
4–6 tablespoons cold water

Filling

1 ⅓ cups sugar
½ cup all-purpose flour
6 cups sour pitted cherries
2 tablespoons butter

Heat oven to 425 degrees Fahrenheit.

In medium bowl, mix 2 cups flour and salt. Cut in shortening, using a pastry blender (or pulling two table knives through ingredients in opposite directions), until particles are the size of small peas. Sprinkle with cold water, 1 tablespoon at a time, tossing with fork until all flour is moistened and pastry almost leaves the side of the bowl (1 to 2 teaspoons more water can be added if necessary).

Gather pastry into a ball. Divide pastry in half and shape into two rounds. Wrap flattened rounds of pastry in plastic wrap; refrigerate about 45 minutes or until dough is firm and cold, yet pliable.

Roll pastry on lightly floured surface, using floured rolling pin, into circle 2 inches larger than an upside-down 9-inch glass pie plate. Fold pastry into fourths and place in pie plate, or roll pastry loosely around rolling pin and transfer to pie plate. Unfold or unroll pastry and ease into plate, pressing firmly against bottom and side and being careful not to stretch pastry, which will cause it to shrink when baked.

In a large bowl, mix sugar and flour. Stir in cherries.

Spoon mixture into pastry-lined pie plate and then cut butter into small pieces and dot them over the cherries. Cover with top pastry that has slits cut in it, then seal and flute. Cover edge with 2- to 3-inch strip of foil to prevent excessive browning; remove foil during last 15 minutes of baking.

Bake 35 to 45 minutes or until crust is golden brown and juice begins to bubble through slits in crust. Cool on cooling rack at least 2 hours before serving.

Strawberry Muffins

½ cup butter
1 cup sugar
2 eggs
2 cups flour
4 teaspoons baking powder
⅔ cup milk
1 ¼ cups strawberries, chopped
Crystallized sugar (to sprinkle on top after baking)

Cream the butter and sugar, then add eggs, flour, baking powder and milk and mix well. Dredge berries in additional flour before adding to mixture to prevent them from sinking to the bottom—a very important step.

Bake in a preheated oven at 350 for 30 minutes. Remove from the oven and sprinkle a little crystallized sugar on top of each muffin.

Hermits

1 ¾ cups all-purpose flour
½ teaspoon baking soda
½ teaspoon salt
1 teaspoon cinnamon
½ teaspoon freshly grated nutmeg
¼ teaspoon ground cloves
½ cup unsalted butter, softened
⅔ cup packed dark brown sugar
1 large egg
¼ cup molasses
½ cup raisins or currants
½ cup chopped walnuts

In a bowl, whisk together the flour, baking soda, salt, cinnamon, nutmeg and cloves. In another bowl with an electric mixer, cream the butter with the brown sugar, beat in the egg and beat in the molasses. Add the flour mixture, beating the mixture until it is just combined, and stir in the raisins and walnuts. Spread the mixture in a buttered and floured 13- by 9-inch baking pan and bake it in the middle of a preheated 350-degree oven for 15 to 20 minutes, or until a tester comes clean.

Let the mixture cool completely in the pan on a rack, and cut it into 24 bars.

Nut Bread

2 cups graham flour
1 cup all-purpose flour
1 cup sugar
4 teaspoons baking powder
2 teaspoons salt
1 ½ cups milk
1 egg, lightly beaten
¼ cup shortening, melted
1 tablespoon molasses
1 teaspoon vanilla extract
1 ½ cups chopped walnuts or pecans
½ cup sweetened dried cranberries

Sift flour, sugar, baking powder and salt into a large bowl; stir to combine. Add milk, egg, shortening, molasses and vanilla extract, stirring just until moistened. Stir in nuts and cranberries.

Pour batter evenly into two greased (13-ounce) coffee cans or into one greased and floured 9- by 5-inch loaf pan.

Bake at 350 degrees for 1 hour and 10 minutes to 1 hour and 15 minutes or until a long wooden pick inserted in center comes out clean. Cool in pan on a wire rack for 10 minutes; remove from pan and cool completely on wire rack.

Apple Cake

½ cup butter, softened
1 cup sugar
2 eggs
¼ teaspoon vanilla
1 ¼ cups all-purpose flour
1 teaspoon baking soda
1 teaspoon ground cinnamon
¼ teaspoon salt
1 ½ cups shredded peeled apples (about 2 medium apples)
½ cup chopped walnuts

Preheat oven to 350 degrees Fahrenheit. Spray 9-inch round cake pan with baking spray and then dust with flour.

In a large bowl, beat butter and sugar with electric mixer on medium speed until light and fluffy. Beat in eggs, one at a time. Stir in vanilla, flour, baking soda, cinnamon and salt. Stir in apples and walnuts. Spoon into a greased and floured pan.

Bake 40 to 45 minutes or until toothpick inserted in center of cake comes out clean. Cool 10 minutes. Remove from pan to cooling rack and cool 10 minutes longer.

Madeleines
These delicate cookies were served in the Spanish Shop at Jordan Marsh.

⅔ cup all-purpose flour, plus more for molds
1 teaspoon baking powder
¼ teaspoon fine sea salt
⅓ cup sugar
Finely grated zest of 1 lemon
2 large eggs, room temperature
1 tablespoon honey
1 teaspoon pure vanilla extract
½ cup unsalted butter, melted and warm, plus unmelted butter for molds
2 tablespoons whole milk

In a medium bowl, whisk together flour, baking powder and salt; set aside. Place sugar and lemon zest in a bowl. Using your fingertips, rub sugar and lemon zest together until sugar is moist and fragrant. Add eggs and whisk until mixture is pale and thickens slightly, about 2 minutes. Whisk in honey and vanilla. Alternatively, this can be done in the bowl of an electric mixer fitted with the whisk attachment. Gently fold in flour mixture in three additions; fold in melted butter until fully incorporated. Stir in milk. Batter should be smooth and shiny.

Press a piece of plastic wrap against the surface of the batter; transfer to refrigerator and let chill at least 1 hour. Butter and flour a large Madeleine pan. Spoon batter into Madeleine pan; transfer to refrigerator for 1 hour. Place a heavy, large baking sheet in oven; preheat oven to 400 degrees. Place Madeleine pan on preheated baking sheet. Bake until golden and big bumps on top spring back when touched,

11 to 13 minutes. Remove pan from oven and immediately release the Madeleines from pan by rapping pan on counter. If any stick, use a butter knife or fingers to help release.

Let cool on a wire rack.

Almond Tosca Bars

⅓ cup butter
⅓ cup sugar
1¾ cups flour
½ cup chocolate morsels
½ cup chopped almonds
½ cup sugar
⅓ cup light cream
¼ cup unsalted butter

Cream the butter and ⅓ cup of sugar. Blend in flour—the mixture will be crumbly. Press into the bottom of an 8- by 8-inch ungreased pan. Bake 12 minutes in a preheated 375-degree oven. Remove and sprinkle with chocolate morsels. Let stand 5 minutes and then spread chocolate.

For the topping: combine chopped almonds, ½ cup of sugar, cream and butter and bring to a boil, letting the mixture boil for 3 minutes. Pour over chocolate and bake 12 minutes until golden.

Cut into squares or bars when cool.

Fudgies

⅔ cup cooking oil
¾ cup unsweetened cocoa
¼ cup cooking oil
2 eggs, unbeaten
2 cups sugar
2½ cups flour, sifted
1 teaspoon baking soda
1 teaspoon salt
1 teaspoon vanilla

1 ½ cups cold water
1 cup chocolate chips
1 cup chopped walnuts

Combine all ingredients, in order given, except for the chocolate chips and walnuts and beat thoroughly. Pour batter into an ungreased 9- by 12-inch pan and spread evenly. Sprinkle the chocolate chips over the batter and then the walnuts. Bake in a preheated oven at 350 degrees for 30 minutes.

Apricot Squares

1 cup sugar
2 cups plus 1 tablespoon sifted flour
¾ cup shortening
1 ⅓ cups shredded coconut
½ cup chopped pecans
1 egg
1 teaspoon vanilla
¼ teaspoon salt
16 ounces apricot jam

Mix all of the ingredients, except for the apricot jam, until it is crumbly. In a well-greased 9- by 9-inch pan, spread one-half of the mixture, pressing it down firmly. Spread the jam over the mixture and then press remaining mixture over the top. Bake in a preheated 350-degree oven for 35 minutes.

Cool and cut into squares.

Cheese Cake Bars

⅓ cup unsalted butter
⅓ cup brown sugar
1 cup flour
½ cup chopped almonds
¼ cup sugar
1 package (8 ounces) cream cheese

1 egg
2 tablespoons milk
1 tablespoon lemon juice
1 teaspoon vanilla

Cream the butter and brown sugar. Add flour and chopped nuts and mix to make a crumbly mixture. Reserve 1 cup for the topping. Press remaining mixture into the bottom of an 8- by 8-inch pan. Bake in a preheated 350-degree oven for 12 to 15 minutes until light brown.

Blend sugar with cream cheese until smooth. Add the egg, milk, lemon juice and vanilla and beat well. Spread over the mixture and spread evenly. Bake in a preheated 350-degree oven for 25 minutes.

Irish Soda Bread

4 cups sifted enriched flour
¼ cup granulated sugar
1 teaspoon salt
1 teaspoon baking powder
¼ cup unsalted butter
2 cups seedless raisins
1 tablespoon caraway seeds (optional)
1 ⅓ cups buttermilk
1 egg
1 teaspoon baking soda

Sift flour, sugar, salt and baking powder in a large bowl. Cut in softened butter with a pastry blender until the mixture is crumbly. Stir in raisins and, if desired, the caraway seeds. Combine buttermilk, egg and baking soda and mix well before pouring into the flour mixture, and then mix until just moistened. Bake in two greased loaf pans, or a round pan, in a preheated 375-degree oven for 45 to 50 minutes until golden brown.

Cheese Biscuits

These savory biscuits were from Jordan Marsh's *Modes & Manners* (February–March 1927) and were available in the Spanish Shop at Jordan Marsh.

1 cup flour
2 teaspoons baking powder
1 teaspoon sugar
1 tablespoon butter
1 cup grated cheddar cheese

Mix all ingredients and roll to a half-inch thickness. Cut with decoratively shaped cookie cutters or score as diamonds with a sharp knife.

Bake in a preheated oven at 375 degrees for 15 to 18 minutes until brown.

CHAPTER 11

THE TAKEOVER BY MACY'S

Jordan Marsh was the one store of its kind in all the world
—Joe Cedrone

○n 1986, the Canadian Campeau Corporation acquired Allied
Stores Corporation, which was reorganized under the merger
agreement. In February 1987, Campeau merged D.M. Read
Company of Bridgeport, Connecticut, into Jordan Marsh and merged
Jordan Marsh Florida with Maas Brothers of Tampa, Florida, as the newly
created Maas Brothers/Jordan Marsh Florida division.

In 1988, Campeau Corporation acquired Federated Department Stores.
To consolidate with Federated Department Stores, Allied's New York
headquarters moved to Cincinnati. Allied Stores included Bon Marché,
Jordan Marsh, Maas Brothers/Jordan Marsh Florida and Stern's, operating
in tandem with Federated Department Stores: Bloomingdale's, Abraham
and Straus, Lazarus, Rich's, Goldsmith's and Burdines.

In 1990, saddled by debt resulting from the highly leveraged Campeau
takeover of Federated Department Stores, both Federated and Allied filed
for bankruptcy reorganization. Campeau Corp. U.S., Inc., was renamed
Federated Stores, Inc. The operations of Jordan Marsh Florida and Maas
Brothers were absorbed by Burdines in 1991.

In 1992, a new public company, Federated Department Stores, Inc.,
was to emerge. The former Allied Stores Corporation was merged into
Federated. A consolidation of the A&S and Jordan Marsh divisions resulted

Rowland Hussey Macy (1822–1877) started a dry goods store in Boston in 1843 and would see business reversals that led him to move and open a store in Haverhill, Massachusetts, in 1851 to serve the mill industry employees of the area. His stores failed, but he learned from his mistakes and made the decision to move in 1858 to New York City, where he established a new store known as R.H. Macy Dry Goods. In 1895, the store was sold to Isidor and Nathan Straus and went on in the twentieth century to become one of the largest department stores in the world.

The Jordan Marsh Company, seen at the corner of Chauncy and Summer Streets, was the epitome of mid-twentieth-century modernism by Perry, Shaw, Kehoe and Dean, with a decided nod to the architecture of old Boston with the use of red brick and Federal Revival window lintels. The brushed steel letters of "Jordan Marsh Company" boldly proclaimed the presence of the oldest department store in Boston, which was eventually to be bought out by Macy's.

in the A&S/Jordan Marsh division, headquartered in Brooklyn, New York. In 1994, the A&S/Jordan Marsh division merged with Macy's East, and the A&S stores were renamed Macy's in 1995. In 1996, Jordan Marsh stores in the Northeast United States, already part of the Macy's East division, were converted to Macy's.

BIBLIOGRAPHY

Benson, Susan Porter. *Counter Cultures: Saleswomen, Managers, and Customers in American Department Stores*. Champaign: University of Illinois Press, 1986.

Bird, William. *Holidays on Display*. New York: Princeton Architectural Press, 2007.

Boston Almanac. Boston: Damrell & Moore and George Coolidge, 1857.

Boston Almanac. Boston: S.N. Dickinson, B.B. Mussey and Thomas Groom, 1847 and 1849.

Boston Daily Globe. "Memorial to Eben D. Jordan: Employees of the House He Founded Join in Honoring the Famous Boston Merchant." October 14, 1895.

Boston Globe. 1872–1995.

Boston Illustrated. Cambridge, MA: James R. Osgood Company, printed by Welch, Bigelow & Co., 1872.

Brisco, Norris Arthur. *Retail Salesmanship*. N.p.: Kessinger Publishing LLC, 2010.

Clark, Barbara. "The Store that Transformed a City." *Barnstable Patriot*, February 19, 2016.

Clark's Boston Blue Book, 1910. Boston: Sampson & Murdock, 1909.

Cohen, Lizabeth. *Consumers' Republic: The Politics of Mass Consumption in Postwar America*. New York: Alfred A. Knopf, 2003.

Edwards, Richard H., Jr. *Tales of the Observer*. N.p.: Jordan Marsh Company, 1950.

Fellow-Workers Directory. Jordan Marsh Company, n.d.

Hill, Edwin C. *The Historical Register: A Biographical Record of the Men of Our Time Who Have Contributed to the Making of America*. New York, 1920.

Jordan Marsh Company. Fortieth Anniversary History, 1851–91. Boston.

Jordan, Marsh Illustrated Catalogue of 1891. N.p.: Dover Publications, 1991.

Jordan Marsh, the Story of a Store: A Brief Record by Word and Picture Showing the Development, Extent, and Convenient Arrangement of New England's Largest Retail Store. Boston: Jordan Marsh Company, 1912.

Leavitt, Michael Bennett. *Fifty Years in the Theatrical Management*. New York: Broadway Publishing Company, 1912.

Look Magazine 23, no. 26, December 22, 1959.

New England Mercantile Union Business Directory. 1847, 1849.

New York Times. "Eben D. Jordan Dead. Senior Member of the Firm of Jordan, Marsh & Co., of Boston. Millionaire, Once a Penniless Boy. Architect of His Own Fortune. Ranked Among Public-Spirited Citizens and Representative Men." November 16, 1895.

———. November 16, 1895.

Nystrom, Paul Henry. *Economics of Retailing*. N.p.: Hard Press Publishing, 2013.

Railey, Julia Houston. *Retail and Romance (1851–1926)*. Boston, 1926.

Rand, John Clark. *One of a Thousand: A Series of Biographical Sketches of One Thousand Representative Men*. Boston: First National Publishing Company, 1890.

Sammarco, Anthony M. *Forest Hills Cemetery*. Charleston, SC: Arcadia Publishing, 2008.

Scrapbook Relating to the Civil War Centennial Exhibit, Jordan Marsh Company. Boston, 1961. State Library of Massachusetts Special Collections.

Sketches of Successful New Hampshire Men. Manchester, NH: John B. Clarke, 1882.

The Talley. Newsletters published by Jordan Marsh Sports Association, 1940–50.

Welcome to Jordan's: A Guide for Jordan Marsh Employees. N.p., 1952.

Whitaker, Jan. *Service and Style: How the American Department Store Fashioned the Middle Class*. New York: St. Martin's Press, 2006.

ABOUT THE AUTHOR

Referred to as the "Balzac of Boston" by the *Boston Globe*, Anthony Mitchell Sammarco is a noted historian and author of over seventy books on the history and development of Boston and other popular topics, and he lectures widely on the history and development of his native city.

He commenced writing in 1995, and his books *Lost Boston*, *The History of Howard Johnson's: How a Massachusetts Soda Fountain Became a Roadside Icon* and *The Baker Chocolate Company: A Sweet History* have all made the bestseller list. *Boston's Back Bay in the Victorian Era*, *Boston's North End* (and *Il North End di Boston* in Italian) and *The Great Boston Fire of 1872* are among his popular books on Boston.

Sammarco is employed at Boston-based Payne/Bouchier Inc., and since 1997, he has taught history at both the Boston University Metropolitan College and the Urban College of Boston, where he was named educator of the year and where he serves on the Leadership Council. His course "Boston's Immigrants" was developed especially for the Urban College and its multicultural and diverse student base, and his book *Boston's Immigrants* was written to highlight the diversity of the city and is used in his course. His course on Boston history at the Boston University Metropolitan College is a very popular one. He has received the Bulfinch Award from the Doric

Dames of the Massachusetts State House; a lifetime achievement award from the Victorian Society, New England Chapter, as well as the Gibson House Museum; the Washington Medal from Freedom Foundation; the Legionnaire Award from the Renaissance Lodge, Sons of Italy; and I Migliori in Mens et Gesta from the Pirandello Lyceum. He was named Dorchester town historian by Raymond L. Flynn, mayor of Boston, for his innovative lecturing and writing in history. He was elected a fellow of the Massachusetts Historical Society, is a member of the Boston Author's Club, a proprietor of the Boston Athenaeum and a member of the St. Botolph Club. In his volunteer work, he is treasurer of the Victorian Society, New England Chapter; a past president of the Bay State Historical League and the Dorchester Historical Society; and served as a corporator of the New England Baptist Hospital for a decade.

He lives in Boston and in Osterville on Cape Cod with Joe Cedrone, Hutchinson, Pasqualina and the girls in the coop.